The New Testament in Current Study

BOOKS BY REGINALD H. FULLER

The Church of Rome, A Dissuasive (with R. Hanson)

The Mission and Achievement of Jesus

The Book of the Acts of God (with G. E. Wright)

What Is Liturgical Preaching?

Luke's Witness to Jesus Christ

The New Testament in Current Study

THE NEW TESTAMENT
IN CURRENT STUDY

Reginald H. Fuller

CHARLES SCRIBNER'S SONS
NEW YORK

ACKNOWLEDGMENTS

The author acknowledges his indebtedness
to the following publishers for permission
to quote from copyright material:

Thomas Nelson & Sons (New York).
Revised Standard Version of the Holy Bible,
copyrighted 1946 and 1952
by the Division of Christian Education
of the National Council of Churches
S.P.C.K. (London, England).
The Gospel According to St. John by C. K. Barrett,
and *Kerygma and Myth,* Vol. I, by R. Bultmann

A. 1.72 [V]

Printed in the United States of America
Library of Congress Catalog Card Number 62-18271
SBN 684-31040-6 (Trade cloth)
SBN 684-12386-X (Trade paper, SL)

● 6191   Chas. Scribners   G-65060   12-1-71   5 4 3 2 1 0

To the DEAN and FACULTY of
the General Theological Seminary
New York

Preface

THIS BOOK consists of lectures delivered to clergy of the Protestant Episcopal Church at the School of the Prophets, San Francisco, in June, 1960. Some of the chapters have been subsequently expanded, and I am indebted to Messrs. Scribner and their readers for comments, criticisms and suggestions.

The dedication to the Dean and Faculty of the General Seminary, New York, is a token of gratitude for their conferral upon me of the honorary degree of Doctor of Sacred Theology shortly before the lectures were delivered.

REGINALD H. FULLER

Contents

Abbreviations

The New Testament in Current Study

I

The New Testament

and Mythology

IN ORDER TO UNDERSTAND the situation in New Testament studies in the year 1940 or thereabouts, we must first take a look at the development of those studies in the period between the two world wars. That period had witnessed two distinct, yet inter-related movements. One was the growth of "form criticism," [1] the other the recovery of biblical theol-

[1] "Form criticism" is not a good translation of *Formgeschichte* (form history), for "criticism" suggests a preoccupation with negative conclusions, whereas the *history* of the tradition is the primary concern of this school. It seeks to see the literature of the New Testament on the background of the historical situations within the church in which that literature took its rise. But the term "form criticism" has become so widely accepted that it would be pedantic to substitute the more correct "form history."

I

ogy. Both of these movements contributed to the recognition of the centrality of the "kerygma"[2] in the New Testament. The New Testament is not the documentation of a general religious experience, but the proclamation of God's eschatological act in the history of Jesus of Nazareth.[3]

All of the New Testament books are focused on this preaching and spring out of it. The Acts of the Apostles is an account of how the sub-apostolic age understood this preaching to have spread from Jerusalem to Rome during the life-time of the apostles. The epistles are *didache* and *paraenesis,* expositions of the doctrinal implications of the message and ethical exhortations indicating the response of Christian obedience which the message requires. The first three, or synoptic, gospels are expansions of the kerygmatic outline, while the fourth gospel is a restatement of the kerygma in a different terminology.

THE RISE OF DEMYTHOLOGIZING

A fresh turning point in New Testament studies began in 1941 with the delivery and circulation in mimeograph form (it was not published in print until after the war), of Dr. Rudolf Bultmann's famous essay, *Neues Testament und*

[2] For the term, see C. H. Dodd, *The Apostolic Preaching and its Development,* London, 1936 (first ed.), Chapter I. Recent criticisms of the modern use of the Greek word to designate the *content* of the Christian message rather than the *activity* of preaching, e.g., by Christopher Evans, *JTS,* n.s., 7, 1956, pp. 25–41, are unconvincing. See James M. Robinson, *A New Quest of the Historical Jesus,* London and Naperville, 1959, p. 41, n. 2.

[3] For a summary of this preaching, see Dodd, *op. cit.* (1944 reprint), p. 17. There were undoubtedly more varieties in the kerygma than Dodd suggests— cf. H. J. Cadbury in *The Background of the New Testament and its Eschatology,* ed., W. D. Davies and D. Daube, Cambridge, 1956, pp. 300ff. But the various forms all preach Christ as God's eschatological act.

Mythologie.[4] This sketched out the program for a new enterprise in New Testament study. Bultmann agreed with the
position of the period between the wars that the New Testament bears witness to the eschatological act of God in the
history of Jesus of Nazareth. But he pointed out that this
act is proclaimed in terms derived from the now obsolete
mythologies of Jewish apocalyptic and Hellenistic gnosticism. The kerygma presupposes an obsolete cosmology—a
three-storied universe (heaven, earth and hell), the intrusion
into earth of spirits and demons from the other spheres; and
their interference with the inner life of man. The Christ event
is presented in terms, first of the Son of man mythology of
Jewish apocalyptic, and later of the gnostic redeemer myth.[5]

It was the merit of the older liberals that they had been
aware of the presence of this mythological element in the
New Testament. But they had sought to meet the difficulty
by *eliminating* the mythological outworks of the kerygma
—virgin birth, empty tomb, literal ascension, etc.—and by
subtly modernizing the rest—incarnation, atonement, Holy
Spirit—into the timeless truths of religion and ethics. Thus
they lost the sense of the New Testament as the proclamation
of the unique eschatological act of God. It was the merit of
biblical theology in the inter-war years that it recovered the
kerygma. Its defect, according to Bultmann, was that it was
content to go on repeating the kerygma in the same language
in which it was presented in the New Testament, mythology
and all.

'In the fulness of time' God sent forth his Son, a pre-existent
divine Being, who appears on earth as a man. He dies the

---

[4] "New Testament and Mythology." See the translation by the present writer in
Kerygma and Myth I, London, 1953, pp. 1–44.
[5] On this, see below, pp. 121 ff.

death of a sinner on the cross and makes atonement for the sins of man. His resurrection marks the beginning of the cosmic catastrophe. Death, the consequence of Adam's sin, is abolished, and the demonic forces are deprived of their power. The risen Christ is exalted to the right hand of God in heaven and made 'Lord' and 'King.' He will come again on the clouds of heaven to complete the work of redemption, and the resurrection and judgement of men will follow. . . . All this is to happen very soon.[6]

But all of this, *said in that way,* is incredible to modern man. The three-storied universe, in which the world of men is subject to invasions from the other stories by spirits and demons is untenable today. The bodily resurrection of Jesus is incredible. The hope of his imminent second coming was not realized. The idea of an atoning death is nonsense. How can the death of a sinless man two thousand years ago have anything to do with the removal of my guilt today? What the liberals failed to see was that the mythology penetrates the whole of the kerygma, its central elements as well as the periphery.

INTERPRETATION, NOT ELIMINATION

Yet Bultmann wants to accept, and wants to get modern man to accept, what the New Testament is trying to proclaim, namely that the Christ event is God's eschatological act in which God has made available for us the new life as a gift. The problem is therefore to remove the mythological language and yet preserve the essential message of the New Testament. It can, Bultmann maintains, be done, but only

[6] *Kerygma and Myth* I, p. 2.

if we *interpret* the mythology, that is to say, if we let it say what it is trying to say: above all, we must not *eliminate* parts of the mythology and rationalize other parts, as the liberals did.

But how is this interpretation to be accomplished? Two considerations point up the way. One lies in the very nature of myth. The other is the fact that the New Testament itself has already begun the process of reinterpreting the mythology.

Classical scholars like W. F. Otto of Königsberg had, prior to Bultmann's essay, been studying the Greek myths as vehicles of a serious understanding of man and his existence. Their purpose, as Otto and his colleagues see it, is not to provide objective descriptions of the world or to relate objective facts, but to convey a particular understanding of man and of his place in the world. Their purpose, in other words, is not cosmological but anthropological, or, as Bultmann prefers to call it, "existential." Thus the very nature of myth itself demands that myth be demythologized: that is, we must, to use it aright, expose its real intention, the understanding of human life which it enshrines, and state its understanding of human life in non-mythological terms.

Secondly, the New Testament itself has started this process of reinterpretation. To begin with, it offers various alternative mythological expressions of the same thing. Christ's death is sometimes called a sacrifice, while at other times it is described as a victory over the powers of evil. These are not complementary objective truths, but alternative proclamations of the significance of Christ's death for human life. Jesus is sometimes called Messiah, at other times the second Adam. One concept is derived from the political and nationalist eschatology of Palestinian Judaism, the other (according to Bultmann) from the oriental myth of the Heavenly Man. They cannot both be objectively true. Then again, the later Pauline and Johannine writings have already begun the process of demythologizing the earlier kerygma. Paul shifts the emphasis of his proclamation from the future expectation of Christ's return on the clouds of heaven to the believer's present life in Christ. John achieves the same shift with his conception of eternal life already here and now present to faith, and of judgment as already accomplished in the word which Jesus brings.

PREVIOUS ATTEMPTS TO DEMYTHOLOGIZE

Next, Bultmann surveys various attempts at demythologizing which have been carried out in the earlier history of theology. The Alexandrian school (Clement, Origen, etc.) tried to overcome mythology by allegorizing it. They read its literal statements as codes for universal truths of religion and ethics. By doing so, however, they forfeited the kerygma as the proclamation of the unique act of God in Christ.

The liberals (Harnack and his school) sought, as we have already indicated, to eliminate the shell and expose the kernel. The shell was the antiquated mythology, the kernel supposedly an idealistic humanitarian and religious ethic. Once again the kerygma was eliminated as the message of God's saving act in Christ.

Their successors, the History of Religions school, such as Troeltsch, represented an advance. They saw that Christianity was not just ethical idealism, but a piety and a cultus. Once more, however, they too eliminated the act of *God*. The mythology became the vehicle for a social religious experience. All three answers, the Alexandrian, liberal, and History of Religions, led to the "dekerygmatizing" of the New Testament. Thus the question remains: can we demythologize the New Testament in such a way as to retain its proclamation of the eschatological act of God in Christ? Bultmann offers in the latter part of his essay some suggestions (he would modestly claim no more) on the lines a genuine demythologizing should take, and two samples of demythologizing. Any genuine interpretation of the New Testament mythology—faithful that is to its true intention—must be an "existential" one, that is to say, the New Testament myths must be interpreted to expose the Christian understanding of human existence which they enshrine. There are two reasons for the selection of an existential interpretation. Partly it arises from the very nature of myth itself, which, as we have seen, is intended to convey a particular understanding of human existence. Partly, too, it is selected because of the prevailing philosophical climate in contemporary Germany. The two samples of demythologizing or interpretation which he offers, are the death and resurrection of Christ.

DEMYTHOLOGIZING FOR TODAY

Thus the second part of the essay deals with the Christian understanding of human existence. Two kinds of self-understanding are contrasted in the New Testament: life outside of faith, and life in faith. The terms sin, flesh, fear (anxiety) and death are mythological descriptions of this kind of existence. In demythologized, existentialist terms, the life of man "outside of faith" means life in bondage to tangible, visible realities, realities which, since they are perishing, drag man down to perdition with them. Life in faith, on the other hand, means abandoning this adherence to visible, tangible realities, and openness to the forgiving grace of God.

It means release from one's own past and openness to God's future. It means therefore our detachment from the world while still living in the world, using the world "as if not":

> From now on, let those who have wives live *as though* they had *none,* and those who mourn *as though* they were *not* mourning, and those who rejoice *as though* they were *not* rejoicing, and those who buy *as though* they had *no* goods, and those who deal with the world *as though* they had *no* dealings with it. For the form of this world is passing away (I Cor. 7:29–31).

This is true eschatological existence. It says what Jewish apocalyptic, with its myth of an imminent end of the world, and what gnosticism, with its myth of the ascent of the individual soul after death to the world of light, are really trying to say. But eschatological existence is not a new "nature" magically conferred. It is not an assured possession. It has constantly to be renewed in decision and obedience. The indicative "thou art" carries with it an imperative "thou shalt." Hence the ethical exhortations of the epistles.

The description of human existence, apart from faith and within faith, has thus been demythologized. But what of the event which makes possible this transition, the Christ event itself?

Like existentialist philosophy, as presented by Heidegger in his book, *Sein und Zeit,*[7] the New Testament speaks of inauthentic and authentic existence. But there is a crucial difference. The secular philosophy assumes that the transition from inauthentic to authentic existence is something man can achieve for himself. This is because the philosophy does not realize, as the New Testament does, the radical fallenness of man; that, as the New Testament mythologi-

[7] Tübingen, 1927. E. tr., *Being and Time,* New York, 1962.

cally expresses it, man is a "sinner." Because of this radical fallenness, every movement of man's will, even his move to get out of his predicament, is still a movement of fallen man. He is therefore incapable of extricating himself from his plight. Only an act from outside of man, from outside of the world and its possibilities, can effect this transition from inauthentic to authentic existence, only an act of God. But this is just what the New Testament proclaims has happened in the Christ event:

> God was in Christ reconciling the world to himself. . . . For our sake he made him to be sin, so that in him we might become the righteousness of God (II Cor. 5:19, 21).

But is this act itself a myth? True, it is proclaimed in mythological terms, for the New Testament speaks of the pre-existence of the redeemer, his incarnation, and subsequent exaltation. It calls him the Messiah and looks for his second coming on the clouds of heaven. All of these ideas are to be found in and are derived from the contemporary mythologies of Jewish apocalyptic and gnosticism. But there is a difference: in the kerygma, the mythological affirmations are attached to a historical person of the recent past, to Jesus of Nazareth. The reason for this is that the mythology is being used, not to describe Jesus objectively, but to affirm his *significance for faith* as the redemptive act of God.

CROSS AND RESURRECTION DEMYTHOLOGIZED

The third part of the essay gives the two samples of demythologized interpretation from the two central elements in the Christ event, the cross and the resurrection.

The New Testament describes the cross in mythological terms. It is the pre-existent, sinless Son of God who is crucified, and his blood is the atoning sacrifice. Again, his death is the triumph over the demonic powers which hold man in bondage. To demythologize the cross, it must be presented, not as an event external to us, but as one which takes place within our own existence. The cross means our being crucified with Christ. To support this interpretation Bultmann quotes those passages from the Pauline epistles which speak of our dying with Christ in baptism (Rom. 6:3ff.) and the passages which exhort the believers to die to sin (Gal. 5:24, 6:14; Phil. 3:10).

Similarly the resurrection is presented in the New Testament as the resuscitation of Jesus' dead body. It is presented as a miraculous proof of the atoning significance of the cross. But you cannot prove one article of faith (the redemptive significance of the cross) by another (the raising of Jesus' dead body). Thus the resurrection is really only a mythological way of proclaiming the saving significance of the cross. As a historical event, all that the historian can affirm is *the Easter faith of the first disciples,* i.e., that they came to believe in Jesus as risen.

The Christ event touches our existence, and therefore ceases to be purely mythological, when it is preached and received in faith, and only then. This preaching and the response of faith are part of the eschatological event, the Christ event, and the Christ event is incomplete without them. The church is the community of those who through the preaching and through faith participate in the eschatological event, and is therefore herself part of the eschatological event.

THE REAL STUMBLING BLOCK

Here then, in significant areas, the kerygma of the New Testament has been demythologized. Is there, asks Bultmann, any mythology left? Some will object that it is mythological to speak of an act of God in any sense at all. But this objection, counters Bultmann, uses the word "mythological" in the old sense. The act of God, as Bultmann has used the term, is not a miraculous, supernatural occurrence. Rather, it is a concrete piece of history, which is otherwise explicable within the ordinary framework of history, though to faith it is perceptible as the eschatological act of God. The Word became flesh (John 1:14). To the outward eye the Christ event is only flesh, as fleshly as any other visible event. But to the eye of faith it is God's eschatological Word. Here is the real paradox of faith, the genuine stumbling block of the Christian message. This stumbling block—as opposed to the adventitious stumbling block of the mythological language—Bultmann will not remove. Demythologizing removes the adventitious stumbling block precisely in order to expose the real stumbling block with brutal clarity. It does so in order to enable modern man to make an authentic decision for or against the kerygma, instead of being prematurely put off by the mythological language and imagery. This is no attempt to water down the kerygma to make it palatable for Jones (or perhaps, we should say, Schmidt) to swallow. Bultmann's difference from the older liberalism (with which his position is sometimes inaccurately confused) and his positive evangelical intention demand frank and ungrudging recognition.

II

For and Against Bultmann

THE YEARS 1941 to 1953 marked the most heated phase of the Bultmann controversy. Naturally, it started in Germany, where, as we have already stated, the essay was circulated in mimeograph form during the Second World War. When printing became possible again with the cessation of hostilities, the controversy spread to other countries. Switzerland, Scandinavia, England and America, France, Belgium and Italy, and even Japan, have taken part. Originally an inner-Lutheran debate, it has engaged the attention of Reformed, Scottish Presbyterian, Anglican and Free Church and even Roman Catholic scholars. Secular philosophers have had their say—for Bultmann's use of Heidegger makes his essay a con-

cern of theirs too. The course of the debate can be followed
in German in the five volumes of *Kerygma und Mythos*.[1]

Here are some of the main points which have arisen in the
debate.

BULTMANN'S POSITIVE CONTRIBUTION

It is generally recognized that Bultmann has rendered a
great service by putting his finger on a real problem for the
church today, one of which theologians were insufficiently
aware during the recovery of biblical theology. That problem
is, how to communicate the Christian message to modern
man in such a way as to challenge him to a genuine decision.
The late Julius Schniewind has given us three examples[2] of
the irrelevance and absurdity of much present-day preaching.
Most clergy of any denomination could parallel them from
their own experience. The first is of an educated lady who,
after listening to a sermon on Genesis 2–3 asked how the sin
of one man so long ago could affect her life today. The second story is of an Ascension Day sermon preached to crowds
of university students near Heidelberg in 1906, which painted
the picture of a literal ascension. The third example was of
an Easter sermon preached by an army chaplain in the First
World War. Although the preacher had said nothing of the
kind, his hearers assumed that he was actually speaking of a
literal resurrection of Christ's earthly body from the grave,
flesh, bones and all.

Nevertheless, many of Bultmann's critics, while agreeing

[1] Ed., H.-W. Bartsch, Hamburg, 1948–55. Selections from Vols. I and II, translated by the present writer, were published by S.P.C.K. in London, 1954. A revised translation of this volume (*Kerygma and Myth* I) is now available here
published by Harper. A second volume of translations, also by the present writer,
from Vols. III–V was published in London, April, 1962 (*Kerygma and Myth* II).

[2] *Kerygma and Myth* I, London, 1954, p. 46.

in principle with the legitimacy and necessity of his proposed task, demur emphatically at some of his methods and conclusions.

SOME CRITICISMS OF BULTMANN

The first important criticism concerns the location of the Christ event, a point urged by both Schniewind and Thielicke.[3] Did it take place "in the years A.D. 1–30," or as some wag has put it, does it take place when Dr. Bultmann ascends the pulpit at 11 a.m. on a Sunday morning? Does it take place in the consciousness of the believer (shades of Schleiermacher!), or does it take place in the combination of the two, preaching of the word and the response of faith? Of course Bultmann admits that the "events of A.D. 1–30" have something to do with kerygma; but, complains Thielicke, these events are only connected "deistically" with the preaching and response. All that the Christ event, as generally understood, has to do with the real thing, the preaching and response of faith, is to "crank up" or spark off the kerygma.

In reply, Bultmann made his point a little clearer, guarding himself from an apparently pardonable misunderstanding. The event of A.D. 1–30 is not merely symbolic of "eternal ideas": the crucifixion is indeed an historical occurrence. It is only because of what happened on the first Good Friday that I can be crucified with Christ. But as a past historical fact the cross is not a redemptive event in its own right: it becomes so only when it is preached and believed in as such. Therefore we cannot say that either the cross in itself or the preaching and the response of faith in themselves are the eschatological event. Rather, the cross plus the preaching

[3] *Kerygma and Myth* I, pp. 78ff. and 138ff.

plus the acceptance of the preaching in faith form as a single complex the eschatological event.

Bultmann's treatment of the resurrection has brought even more trenchant criticism, particularly from Karl Barth.[4] Here we should remind ourselves that whether we agree with Bultmann or not, the resurrection itself is not in any case a historical event in the ordinary sense of the word. That is to say, it cannot be proved or established by the ordinary methods of historical criticism. But how then is it to be classified? Bultmann, it will be remembered, says that it is a mythological way of proclaiming the redemptive significance of the cross. All that actually happened or that can be proved to have happened over and above the cross, on the first Easter day, was the rise of the Easter faith in the first disciples. Against this, both Schniewind and Thielicke insist that, according to the New Testament, the resurrection was an event which happened over and above the event of Good Friday. There was a transaction between God and Jesus as well as between God and the disciples.

Does this therefore mean that the resurrection is after all to be classified as a historical event? Clearly, not in the ordinary sense of the word. Jesus was only revealed to chosen witnesses, who came to *believe* in him as risen. If therefore by "historical" we mean "verifiable" or "demonstrable by historical criticism" the resurrection itself, apart from the rise of the Easter faith, is not historical. The Easter faith however, according to the New Testament, did not arise in a vacuum, but was the response to what it understood to be certain prior actions of God himself. To begin with, Christ "appeared" to his disciples. The Greek word for this is *ophthe,* which denotes that God revealed Jesus to

---

[4] In *Rudolf Bultmann, Ein Versuch, ihn zu verstehen,* Zurich, 1953. E. tr. in *Kerygma and Myth* II, pp. 83–132.

the disciples as risen. And the revelation pointed back to another act of God prior to that, the act by which God had "raised" Jesus. Thus the New Testament understands the resurrection not merely as a mythological statement of the saving significance of the cross, but as an occurrence between God and Jesus. In the resurrection God took the existence of Jesus out of the flux of history into his own eternity, so that he becomes the permanently available eschatological event, to be proclaimed in the kerygma. Bultmann has been accused of implying that Jesus was merely "raised into the kerygma," that he becomes risen (mythologically speaking) only when and insofar as he is preached as the redemptive event. The New Testament, however, proclaims that Jesus was raised before he entered into the kerygma, and that he enters into the kerygma precisely because God has first raised him: "If Christ has not been raised, then our preaching (kerygma) is in vain and your faith is in vain" (I Cor. 15:14). Paul here clearly states that it is not our kerygma or faith which creates the "resurrection" of Christ, but the prior act of God's having raised Jesus that makes the kerygma and faith what they are.

Again, it must be insisted that the resurrection of Christ does not occur first, or exclusively, in my existence, in my rising with Christ. Christ is the firstfruits of them that slept, the first to achieve, through the prior act of God, the "eschatological break-through," and it is only because he has achieved it first that we can achieve it too. His resurrection, as Barth has aptly phrased it, is prior to all other resurrections, including existential ones.

THE RIGHT WING CRITICS

So much for the main criticisms of Schniewind, Thielicke and Barth. We turn now to Bultmann's right wing critics, the representatives of Lutheran orthodoxy. At the 1952 assembly of the bishops of the United Lutheran Church of Germany [5] a pastoral letter was issued condemning the theology of demythologizing (Bultmann was not mentioned by name) as "false doctrine." This stand of the bishops was buttressed by an officially sponsored volume of essays edited by Ernst Kinder.[6] Lutheran orthodoxy's basic charge against Bultmann is his denial of what these theologians call the "objective factualness" of the redemptive events, i.e., the incarnation, atonement, resurrection, ascension and second coming. Friedrich Gogarten's *Demythologizing and History* [7] is largely a defense of Bultmann against their criticisms. Further account of the Lutheran position will be found in H.-W. Bartsch's supplementary volume to *Kerygma und Mythos I–II*.[8] Their accusation that Bultmann denies the objective factualness of the redemptive events was already foreshadowed in Thielicke's charge that for him everything seems to happen "in the human consciousness." [9] The facts of salvation are not objectively redemptive in themselves, but become so only when I believe in them and they transform my existence. Bultmann recognizes exclusively the *pro me:* the Lutherans are concerned to give due recognition to the *pro se.* This has proved to be the most vitriolic part of the demythologizing controversy. While the Lutherans have flung charges of heresy at Bultmann and his dis-

---

[5] VELKD (Vereinigte evangelische Lutherische Kirchen Deutschlands) is the more strictly confessional grouping of Lutheran provincial churches, distinct from the wider grouping, EKiD, Evangelische Kirche in Deutschland, which includes churches which are Lutheran, Reformed and United.

[6] *Ein Wort Lutherischer Theologie zur Entmythologisierung,* Munich, 1952. The essays by Ellwein, Kinder and Künneth have been published in E. tr. by Carl E. Braaten and Roy A. Harrisville in *Kerygma and History,* Nashville, 1962.

[7] London, 1955, translated by N. H. Smith from the German entitled *Entmythologisierung und Kirche,* Stuttgart, 1953.

[8] E. tr., *Kerygma and Myth* II, pp. 1–82.   [9] *Kerygma and Myth* I, p. 148.

ciples, the latter in turn, by appealing to Luther and Melanchthon, have accused the former of betraying the Reformation.
For demythologizing, the Bultmannians claim, is the carry-
ing out of the Reformation principles of *sola fide* in the
sphere of epistemology.[10] Melanchthon's dictum is quoted,
Hoc est Christum cognoscere, beneficia eius cognoscere, "to
know Christ is to know his benefits." It would seem that
much of this is merely a battle of words, generating more
heat than light. This is particularly true of the discussion
about the meaning of "objectivity." When the Lutherans
speak of "objectivity" the Bultmannians charge them with
intruding into theology an alien philosophical framework
of thought, the subject-object pattern. This pattern was, on
the one hand, unknown before Descartes (and therefore
unknown to Luther) and, on the other hand, has since
become obsolete. It is true of course that the incarnation, etc.,
are not objective in the Cartesian sense of the word. The
only "objective" facts in that refined philosophical sense
are these: Jesus of Nazareth was born at some time, pre-
sumably in the reign of Caesar Augustus; he was executed
one Friday at passover time during the procuratorship of
Pontius Pilate in Judea; and his disciples came to believe a
day or two later that he had been raised from the dead. Incarnation, atonement, and resurrection are affirmations of
faith, faith that the objective events just mentioned have
redemptive significance. The events themselves cannot be
proved objectively to have that significance. They do not
have that significance for anyone outside of the faith relationship. But faith (in the New Testament and Christian sense
of the word) cannot understand itself as reading into the
facts a significance that was not already there prior to faith.
Faith knows in the moment it comes into being that what it

[10] *Kerygma and Myth* I, pp. 210f.

believes was already there prior to itself: it believes only because of that priority. Anglicans would find an analogy here with the sacrament of the Holy Communion. The bread and wine are not "objectively" the body and blood of Christ, if by "objective" we mean "verifiably so by chemical or psychological analysis." Only faith knows them to be the body and blood of Christ. But faith also knows that they do not become the body and blood of Christ as a result of faith itself. Faith knows that the body and blood of Christ were there prior to itself, and that it only recognizes what was there before it came to believe. It is the priority (rather than the "objectivity" in a Cartesian sense) of the redemptive act to faith that the orthodox Lutherans are trying to assert. It is unfortunate that they have exposed themselves to misunderstanding and criticisms by using the questionable word "objective." But their use of it springs from a legitimate concern which in some moments (for instance when defending themselves against the charge of locating the redemptive event exclusively in the preaching and its acceptance in faith) even Bultmann and his disciples apparently share.

THE LEFT WING CRITICS

At the opposite extreme stand the left-wing critics, the Swiss "liberal" theologians, led by Fritz Buri,[11] and together with them the German existentialist philosopher, Karl Jaspers,[12] whose existentialism is of an agnostic, humanist

[11] In the Swiss context "liberal" means the school which, following Albert Schweitzer, finds the clue to the history of dogma in the delay of parousia, and the permanent essence of Christianity in "reverence for life." See Martin Werner's *The Formation of Christian Dogma*, London, New York, 1957.

[12] Jaspers is here included among the critics of the left. At the same time, however, it needs to be noted that he also criticizes Bultmann from the right, viz.,

type, though not atheistic. These critics accuse Bultmann of not going far enough in his demythologizing. In retaining the act of God he has left a remnant of mythology. They therefore demand the "dekerygmatizing" of Christianity, the removal of the proclamation of the act of God in Jesus Christ altogether. This proclamation, for them, is merely an outworn symbol of the transition from inauthentic to authentic existence, achieved simply by human decision (which, in Buri at any rate, can be understood in faith, paradoxically, as the act of God). It is for this retention of the act of God in Christ—and particularly the exclusive insistence that it is through Christ alone that the transition is effected, the *sola gratia* of the Lutheran Reformation, that Jaspers accuses Bultmann of "orthodoxy" and "illiberality"(!). In defense, Bultmann and his disciples insist on the evangelical purpose behind demythologizing. It does not spring from a purely rationalistic, intellectual criticism of the kerygma. Its intention is to set free the New Testament message of God's act in Christ in all its naked clarity and to make it audible in the modern world. Buri and Jaspers would compel Bultmann to forsake his basic goal, which is to exegete the *New Testament*.

THE HERMENEUTICAL PROBLEM

This brings us to a subject which has engaged much attention in the more recent phase of the demythologizing controversy, namely the problem of hermeneutics. This problem had been largely neglected, not only during the form-critical

---

for going too far. Not only does Jaspers feel that Bultmann goes too far in eliminating the sense of mystery from "religion" in the interests of a shallow rationalism: he also criticizes him for showing too much deference to the "scientific world view." Jaspers believes that there is no such thing.

period, but also, more surprisingly at first sight, in the biblical revival that followed. Hermeneutics means the science of interpreting documents, particularly ancient documents, in such a way that they speak relevantly to present-day man. In order to hear what the document is saying we must approach it with the right questions. The right question with which to approach the New Testament, Bultmann maintains, is the question of human existence, a question motivated by what St. Augustine called man's *cor inquietum,* his restless heart. The New Testament message is seen as the answer to this quest, and is to be expounded as such. Now, that the New Testament offers an answer to man's existential question is not to be denied, and that the New Testament message comes to life when it is seen as such an answer is equally true. But is the New Testament message *only* and exclusively an answer to man's existential question? If it is interpreted as such, are there not many features in the message which, because they cannot be interpreted as part of the answer to man's existential question, will have to be eliminated? Bultmann repeatedly claims that demythologizing aims at interpreting (existentially) the New Testament message. May it not be that in practice, and despite this oft-repeated intention, he does eliminate those parts of the New Testament message which are not susceptible of existential interpretation? Such elements are, or may be, the doctrine of creation (apart from my receiving my own individual existence from the Creator), the doctrine of providence, man as a reality, both body and soul, redemption as a corporate process, and the church as the body of Christ, not simply the place where the individual hears and responds to the New Testament message. When accused by American critics, such as Amos N. Wilder and Sherman Johnson, of having no specific doctrine of the church, Bultmann and his disciples reply by pointing to the statement in the original essay that the church is part of the eschatological phenomenon (see above, p. 10). So far, so good, but does this actually mean any more than that the church is the place where the eschatological word is proclaimed and heard and believed? If so, then the concept of the church has been individualized: it becomes merely a juxtaposition of individual preachers and believers. Here, perhaps, we see the heritage of Lutheran pietism, which comes to Bultmann directly, as well as *via* his dependence on existentialist philosophy. He and his followers would do well to be a little more self-critical here. Bultmann can also say very little about the futurist eschatology, except that the future, a kind of will-o'-the-wisp, always just ahead of us, never within our grasp, somehow qualifies the present. He cannot hold out any real content in Christian hope, for this would be "false objectifying." [13] He cannot really say anything about the destiny either of the individual or of the cosmos, even in the most refined theological terms. Indeed, the whole New Testament conception of cosmic redemption refuses to pass through the sieve of existential interpretation, and must therefore in practice be eliminated. The same applies to the "myths" of Christ's pre-existence, the virgin birth and the second coming. These too have a significance which transcends the existence of the individual.

Sherman Johnson and Amos N. Wilder [14] have devoted a good deal of attention to the place of myth in religious language. Myth, they assert, is an indispensable vehicle of

[13] Cf. his essay in *Glauben und Verstehen* III, Tübingen, 1960, pp. 81–90, entitled "Die Christliche Hoffnung und das Problem der Entmythologisierung." This was Bultmann's contribution to a radio discussion in Germany on the theme of the Evanston Assembly of the World Council of Churches in 1954.

[14] Amos N. Wilder, *New Testament Faith for Today*, New York, 1955, Ch. II, "The Language of Faith," pp. 38–71; Sherman Johnson, *ATR*, 36, I (Jan., 1954), "Bultmann and the Mythology of the New Testament," pp. 29–47.

religious truth, without which all religion, including the Christian gospel, would be condemned to silence. Mythical language is not accurate, scientific description, but is allusive, poetical and imaginative. It is symbolic, and is suggestive of truth, viz., of transcendental truth, which cannot be conveyed by the use of ordinary descriptive, objectifying language. Truths of this order cannot be communicated by any other language, e.g., by the discursive language of science. Myth *must* therefore be used in communicating and expressing Christian truth. At the same time these writers readily admit that side by side with this continued use of myth there must constantly go its more prosaic interpretation in preaching, teaching and apologetic in order to guard against a literal, objectifying misunderstanding of mythical speech. Yet it is continually necessary to return to the mythical language as the only language capable of expressing the religious truth in all its profundity. This is necessary particularly in the language of liturgy—a point which Bultmann himself would hardly contest.[15]

There must then, it is admitted, be interpretation of the Christian myths all the time. But how are they to be interpreted? Bultmann says, existentially. This, as we have seen, is helpful with those aspects of the New Testament language, of those myths which concern our appropriation of the saving act of God in Christ. But when it comes to speaking of the saving act itself, the use of existentialist interpretation results in the discarding or ignoring of some myths, and in the inadequate interpretation of others. Therefore, despite Bultmann's professed intention, we get elimination of significant areas of the New Testament proclamation. As we have seen, we hear nothing about the church as a corporate fellowship, or of the future, both cosmic and indi-

[15] See, e.g., *Kerygma and Myth* I, pp. 102f.

vidual. Against this it must be insisted that, true to the professed program of demythologizing, *all* of the New Testament mythology must be retained, and all must be interpreted. And where the existential interpretation is inapplicable, some other kind of interpretation must be discovered. Only so will we avoid taking the witness of the New Testament to the Christ event à la carte.[16]

---

[16] Cf. *The New Testament and Mythology,* Burton H. Throckmorton, Jr., Philadelphia, 1959, pp. 147–206. The present writer is indebted to this work in the preceding paragraphs.

III

The New Quest
of the Historical Jesus

AT THIS POINT we enter what has come to be called the "post-Bultmannian" phase of New Testament study. The new phase was inaugurated by a lecture delivered in 1953 at a gathering of former students of Dr. Bultmann at Marburg. It was given by one of his leading pupils, Ernst Käsemann, now at Tübingen, and was entitled "The Problem of the Historical Jesus." [1] Käsemann proposed to re-open the long-neglected concern with the Jesus of History. The challenge was taken up by others, notably by Ernst Fuchs and Günther Bornkamm. A series of articles by Bultmann's pupils and others have been appearing since 1954 in the periodical, *Zeitschrift für Theologie und Kirche*. These

[1] E. tr. in *Essays on New Testament Themes,* London and Naperville, 1964, pp. 15–47.

discussions have borne positive fruit in two new presenta-
tions of Jesus and his history, the first to emerge from the
Bultmann school since 1926,[2] Günther Bornkamm's *Jesus
von Nazareth* (1956),[3] and Conzelmann's article, "Jesus
Christus" in the third edition of the German encyclopedia,
Religion in Geschichte und Gegenwart (1959). The course
of the debate has been ably summarized and evaluated for
English-speaking readers by James M. Robinson in his book,
A New Quest of the Historical Jesus.[4]

THE ABANDONMENT OF THE OLD QUEST

As the title of Robinson's report reminds us, there had
been an old quest, pursued mainly by German scholars from
the latter years of the eighteenth century down to about 1900.
The history of the old quest was monumentally related in
Albert Schweitzer's classic, *The Quest of the Historical
Jesus.*[5] The chief motivation behind the older quest was to
get back behind the orthodoxy of the church to the original
teachings of Jesus and thus acquire a corrective to the church's
version of Christianity. Fortunately for itself, this quest co-
incided with the development of the historico-critical
method, which promised objective scientific results. Harnack's famous *What is Christianity?* [6] represents the fine

[2] Bultmann's own *Jesus.* E. tr., *Jesus and the Word,* New York, 1934.

[3] E. tr., *Jesus of Nazareth,* New York, 1960.

[4] See above, p. 2, n. 2. An enlarged edition has since appeared in German
under the title *Kerygma und historischer Jesus,* Zurich, 1960.

[5] London, 1910. The title of the German original, published in 1906, was
Von Reimarus zu Wrede, these being the names of the first and last scholars
whose reconstructions of the historical Jesus are reported by Schweitzer.

[6] London and New York, 1901. The German original was entitled, *Das Wesen
des Christentums,* Berlin, 1900. The English edition has been reissued in a paper-
back with a foreword by R. Bultmann, New York, 1957.

flower of this enterprise, with its attractive portrait of Jesus as the teacher of the fatherhood of God and the brotherhood of man—a far cry from the supernatural figure of the traditional faith of the church, the agent of salvation and the founder of the sacramental institution. Unfortunately, however, just as the quest had seemingly attained its goal, it took an embarrassing turn. By the very application of the historico-critical method in all its scientific rigor, William Wrede and Julius Wellhausen between them demonstrated that the Jesus of history, as reconstructed by the liberal scholars, was not a scientific product after all. Wrede showed that St. Mark's gospel is in fact a highly theological document, not the simple life of Jesus it had been taken to be. Wellhausen extended Wrede's insight to all the synoptic gospels. All of them were records of the church's faith, rather than biographies of Jesus. A few years later Wellhausen's suggestions were taken up and given a much firmer basis by the form critics [7] in a series of studies devoted to the pre-literary history of the gospel material. It was shown that the gospels were composed of originally isolated units of material, all of them shaped not for historical record, but to meet the day-to-day needs of the church in its preaching and teaching and other activities. The material was in other words shaped for "kerygmatic" rather than for historical purposes. K. L. Schmidt also showed that Mark had arranged his material (and the same would be true of the other gospels) not in historical order, but on topical, topographical and theological grounds. This meant that the reconstruction of the historical Jesus in a modern biographi-

[7] M. Dibelius, *Die Formgeschichte des Evangeliums*, Tübingen, 1919 (E. tr., *From Tradition to Gospel*, London and New York, 1934); K. L. Schmidt, *Der Rahmen der Geschichte Jesu*, Berlin, 1919; R. Bultmann, *Die Geschichte der synoptischen Tradition*, Göttingen, 1921 (E. tr. of the third edition, 1957, in preparation); M. Albertz, *Die synoptischen Streitgespräche*, Berlin, 1921.

cal sense was impossible. We do not have the sources for the task. Two famous quotations express this:

> We can, strictly speaking, know nothing of the personality of Jesus.[8]

> It seems then that the form of the earthly no less than of the heavenly Christ is for the most part hidden from us. For all the inestimable value of the gospels, they yield us little more than a whisper of His voice; we trace in them but the outskirts of His ways.[9]

Nor was it long before the quest of the historical Jesus was discovered to be unnecessary. Contemporary with the form critical movement came the rise of the so-called dialectical theology, pre-eminently linked with the name of Karl Barth. Following the lead of Kierkegaard, the dialectical theologians contended that to concern oneself at all with the problem of the historical Jesus was to deny the true nature of faith. Faith was a one hundred percent risk, a leap in the dark. We hear in the church the proclamation of the Word which announces Christ as the redemptive act of God. The proclamation challenges us to a groundless either/or decision. To try to prove that Jesus is the redemptive act of God is to seek a false security. Or, as Martin Kähler had powerfully urged in 1892,[10] to seek for the so-called historical

[8] R. Bultmann, *Jesus and the Word,* New York, 1936, p. 9.

[9] R. H. Lightfoot, *History and Interpretation in the Gospels,* London and New York, 1935, p. 225. Lightfoot later complained that this passage had been widely misunderstood by his critics (*The Gospel Message of St. Mark,* Oxford, 1950, p. 103n.). He points out here that the words in question are in fact "almost a quotation from Job 26:14," and are intended to draw out the contrast between "the comparatively small knowledge . . . that is at present available to man" and "the boundless immensity which is quite beyond his grasp." The main point, however, still stands: our knowledge of the historical Jesus is "comparatively small."

[10] *Der sogenannte historische Jesus und der biblische, geschichtliche Christus.*

Jesus was to tie faith to the shifting results of historical criticism, so that the simple believer could never know what to believe. The object of faith was not the historical Jesus, however reconstructed, but the kerygma, the Word preached by the apostles, recorded in the New Testament, and continued in the church. The history of Jesus was irrelevant for faith.

There is an analogy between the dialectical position and the school of Oxford scholars who are pupils of R. H. Lightfoot,[11] from whose Bampton lectures we have just quoted. Here we find, transposed into a high Anglican key, the same sort of attitude. These scholars too can be quite radical, even skeptical, about the Jesus of history, yet completely unperturbed so far as their Christian faith is concerned. For them the object of faith is not the Jesus of history, but the faith of the church, the Christian creeds. The typological treatment of the gospels as practiced by Austin Farrer tends in the same direction.[12] For Dr. Farrer the gospels are in no sense historical records of the life of Jesus, but elaborate typological patterns created by the church (albeit under inspiration). This does not, however, undermine faith, since what we believe is the Catholic creeds and not the historical Jesus.

THE REASONS FOR THE NEW QUEST

Why then this renewal of concern with the historical Jesus? It has been touched off largely by the program of

---

This essay, born of a controversy with Wilhelm Herrmann, was little regarded at the time, but has since come into its own. It was re-issued in 1953 (Munich).

[11] See the essays by C. F. Evans and D. E. Nineham in *Studies in the Gospels*, ed., D. E. Nineham, Oxford, 1955, pp. 37–53 and 223–239.

[12] *A Study in St. Mark*, London, 1951, and New York, 1952. Also *St. Mark and St. Matthew*, London, 1954.

demythologizing (see Chapters I and II). The "myths" of the kerygma—pre-existence, incarnation, atonement, resurrection, ascension, etc.—are all interpretative rather than objective statements. What they interpret is precisely the *history* of Jesus. Bultmann made a great point of this when he distinguished between the kerygma and mythology pure and simple:

> The event of Christ is of a wholly different order from the cult myths of Greek or Hellenistic religion. Jesus Christ is certainly presented as the Son of God, a pre-existent divine being, and therefore to that extent a mythical figure. But he is also a concrete figure of history—Jesus of Nazareth. His life is more than a mythical event; it is a human life which ended in the tragedy of crucifixion.[13]

If this statement is taken seriously, it means that we must modify the position, shared elsewhere by Bultmann himself, that a concern for the historical Jesus is irrelevant for faith. Otherwise we shall be in danger of lapsing into a "kerygma-theological docetism." [14] We shall be left with the mythological interpretation of an *x* of which we can know nothing, or only the bare fact that he was. For Kierkegaard that was enough, and for Bultmann that seems generally to be enough. But as the present writer maintained (the words were written shortly before Käsemann launched the post-Bultmannian quest) in *The Mission and Achievement of Jesus*,[15] we must at least try to show that the history of Jesus can bear the weight of its post-Easter interpretation in the kerygma. Not that we should seek to prove that the keryg-

[13] *Kerygma and Myth* I, p. 34.
[14] N. A. Dahl, "The Problem of the Historical Jesus," in *Kerygma and History* (above, p. 17, n. 6).
[15] London, 1954, pp. 14ff.

ma's interpretation of his history is true. Only faith can decide that. Nor should we hope to demonstrate that Jesus' understanding of his own history was *identical* with the kerygma's interpretation of it. But at least we have a right to demand that there should be a *continuous frame of reference* between Jesus and the kerygma.

Now Käsemann and his colleagues have been able to seize upon certain features of Bultmann's scholarship which had often been overlooked. Side by side with an apparently almost total skepticism about the historical Jesus there are other statements which would seem more hopeful. He does insist, as we have seen, that the kerygma is the interpretation of a real historical person. Moreover he *did* write *Jesus and the Word,* which, despite the quotation on page 9 (above, page 28), contained 226 pages about Jesus' message and teachings. He also wrote 30 pages on Jesus in his *Theology of the New Testament,*[16] not all of which are negative. It is true that Jesus is there relegated to the "presuppositions" for the kerygma, and that the space allotted to him compares somewhat staggeringly with the three hundred-odd pages on Paul, but the significant thing is that Bultmann could write as many as thirty pages about Jesus' message and his ethical demand. These should offer important clues to Jesus' own understanding of his mission. It is true that we have Bultmann's oft-quoted statement that the life of Jesus was "not messianic," though even here it is important to note the qualification he adds, to the effect that by "not messianic" he is not speaking of the ultimate significance of Jesus' history and person for faith, but only of Jesus' own non-use of any current Messianic categories, whether literally or spiritualized, in the interpretation of his person. Yet, what has less frequently been noticed, Bultmann also

[16] Vol. I, London and New York, 1952.

avers that "Jesus' call to decision implies a Christology."[17]
We shall return to this admission later. Meanwhile, let us
simply note that Bultmann *can* make some positive statements about the historical Jesus. There would seem to be
some lines therefore in Bultmann's thought which suggest
that concern with the historical Jesus is both legitimate and
possible. What he was ruling out of court was the wrong
kind of concern with the historical Jesus, the attempt to
reconstruct a continuous biography of the modern kind,
tracing Jesus' psychological development, and the use of
this reconstruction to read off from it what Christian faith
ought to be.

THE POSSIBILITY OF A NEW QUEST

It still remains true, even for Käsemann and his colleagues,
that the gospels are kerygmatic in character: they are written not to impart historical information about Jesus, but to
proclaim him as the act of God. Nor, despite the claims of
Ethelbert Stauffer to the contrary,[18] do we have any "new"
sources to enable us to resume the quest. The "new" sources
brought forward by Stauffer consist mainly of Talmudic
references to Jesus, which have no independent source value,
but are simply counter-propaganda reflecting current Christian tradition. The other materials to which Stauffer appeals
—our more recently acquired knowledge of Palestinian
topography, social customs and daily life (Renan's "fifth
gospel"), together with the Qumran documents—have an
indirect background value, but are in no sense new sources
for the life of Jesus. But form criticism itself, though its
results are often thought to be largely negative, does in fact
provide valuable criteria to enable us to distinguish between

[17] *Theology of the New Testament* I, pp. 27, 43.
[18] *Jesus and His Story*, London, 1960.

the authentic sayings of Jesus and creations of the post-
Easter church. Thus we can, for historical purposes, eliminate from the sayings of Jesus anything which clearly presupposes the post-Easter situation, and which reflects the
faith of the post-Easter church. For here the presumption
is that their *Sitz im Leben,* their creative milieu, is in the
life of the church, and not in the life of Jesus. Secondly, we
can eliminate any material which can be paralleled in contemporary Judaism, for here too the presumption is that
the sayings in question have (historically speaking) been
erroneously attributed to Jesus. This material would include
sayings which are paralleled in Jewish apocalyptic and in
Rabbinic tradition. Of course these methods are not fool-
proof, and one cannot help feeling that German scholars
often proceed as if they were. They yield no complete
certainty, for on some points Jesus *could* have agreed with
the post-Easter church: but usually, in a saying of this class,
the post-Easter situation is clearly reflected. Jesus might
also have quoted or used with approval Rabbinic teaching.
The most we can claim for this method of elimination is
that it provides a safer course than Stauffer's principle of
in dubio pro tradito. It may result in a reduction of the
available historical data, but at least it should be reliable
enough as far as it goes: and actually it turns out that it
does go far enough for our purposes. Finally, any saying of
Jesus, if it is authentic, should exhibit Aramaic features, and
if it has the structure of Aramaic poetry [19] this increases the
presumption that the saying is authentic. Of course the
earliest Aramaic-speaking church could also have used poetic
forms, and certainly its creation would undoubtedly exhibit
Aramaic linguistic features, just as the authentic logia of
Jesus. It is the failure to observe this that renders Joachim

[19] See C. F. Burney, *The Poetry of Our Lord,* Oxford, 1925.

Jeremias' study of the words over the bread and cup at the Last Supper [20] so inconclusive. What he claims for Jesus could equally be the creations of the earliest Aramaic-speaking church. Hence this criterion of Aramaic linguistic features cannot be used alone, but can only serve as a support and check for the two criteria mentioned earlier. But the linguistic criterion has special value in enabling us to eliminate later additions to logia. This is especially true of the parables, where it is quite easy to peel off the later interpretations and applications of the church.[21]

WHAT CAN BE KNOWN OF JESUS

In his article on "Jesus Christus" (see above, p. 26), Hans Conzelmann has summarized the material which passes these criteria. Jesus proclaimed the Reign of God. This Reign, while future, was effectively engaging men already in the present in the word of Jesus himself. It demands decision, response, acceptance of the challenge. It is making itself felt in advance in the words and works of Jesus, so that men's lives here and now are "decisively qualified" in the present by the future Reign of God. At this point Ernst Fuchs [22] contributes the important addition that Jesus' gracious activity in eating with publicans and sinners (what Fuchs calls Jesus' conduct, *Verhalten*) is a special concentration of the redeeming activity of the Reign of God already making itself felt in advance. We might add too that Jesus'

[20] J. Jeremias, *Die Abendmahlsworte Jesu*, Göttingen, 1949 (E. tr., *The Eucharistic Words of Jesus*, by A. Ehrhardt, Oxford, 1955).

[21] See C. H. Dodd, *The Parables of the Kingdom*, London, 1935 (rev. ed., New York, 1961); and J. Jeremias, *The Parables of Jesus*, London, New York, 1954 (E. tr. of *Die Gleichnisse Jesu*, Zurich, 1954).

[22] See his article, "Die Frage nach dem historischen Jesus," *ZThK*, 53, 1956, pp. 210–229. E. tr. in *Studies of the Historical Jesus*, London and Naperville, 1964, pp. 11–31.

healings and exorcisms point in the same direction. Jesus'
eschatology implies a present confrontation with the future
Reign of God.

The ethic of Jesus points in the same direction. Jesus
demands absolute, radical obedience to the will of God,
sweeping away all qualifications and evasions ("You have
heard that it was said . . . but I say"). In Jesus' ethic there
is an immediate confrontation with the demanding God.

The teaching of Jesus about God (Conzelmann calls it
his "cosmology") and his providential care (e.g., Matt.
6:19–34) has similar implications. Here Jesus confronts men
with God's direct lordship over human life, which rules out
anxiety. We might also include under the rubric of Jesus'
teaching on God what he says about faith. Gerhard Ebeling
has paid particular attention to this subject.[23] Faith is not a
subjective attitude of the soul, but being on the receiving
end of the divine action. Faith implies an act of God at the
other end. Ebeling calls attention to Hans Schlier's remarkable article on "Amen" in the *Theologisches Wörterbuch*
(Vol. I). Whereas the Jew *concluded* his prayer to God with
Amen, thus expressing his faith that God would act, Jesus
prefaces his words with an "Amen," thus denoting that
prior to his utterance there is his total engagement to the act
of God, of which his words thus become the channel. As
Schlier pertinently remarks, "Amen I say unto you" includes
the whole of Christology in a nutshell.

Günther Bornkamm [24] can also speak of a general impression made by Jesus in the gospels which is quite independent

---

[23] *Word and Faith,* London, 1963, pp. 201–246 (German, 1958); pp. 288–304
(German, 1959). He has also written a full-length work on the subject, *The
Nature of Faith,* London and Philadelphia, 1961 (German, 1959).

[24] *Jesus of Nazareth,* Ch. III.

of the authenticity of this or that particular saying. We are, he says, impressed by Jesus' humble submission to God on the one hand, and his tremendous sense of authority expressed both in word and in deed on the other. Jesus is always master of every situation. His gracious service of man is combined with a penetrating insight into human motives and a radical judgment of their behavior ("He knew what was in man," says the fourth gospel in an editorial comment which is nevertheless completely justified by Jesus' history). Yet this same judgment of men is combined with the acceptance of sinners and their forgiveness. There is nothing in this portrait, says Bornkamm, which could have been read out of or created either by the Messianic expectations of pre-Christian Judaism or by the post-Easter Christology of the church. In fact, it is just these elements which tend to be toned down in the later strata of the gospels. Yet at the same time the impression survives all the way through, even down to the fourth gospel. Here is an encounter with Jesus independent of the kerygma (though of course it has been filtered through the kerygma). It is often said, both by radicals and conservatives, that you cannot get back behind the apostolic witness. In a sense this is true: all we know of Jesus is through the apostolic witness. Yet the techniques of historical, literary and form criticism do enable us to dig through the apostolic witness and come to a pre-Easter stratum which their witness has taken up and used. Thus, as James M. Robinson claims,[25] we have for the first time since the apostolic age a second line of encounter with Jesus additional to the kerygma. It is true of course that the gospels are kerygmatic in intention, not historical or biographical, and that in using them in this way we are using them in a way for which they were not originally intended. But

[25] *A New Quest of the Historical Jesus,* p. 90.

in the service of the kerygma the Evangelists actually use authentic traditions and logia of Jesus, and if they contain such authentic memories, it is certainly legitimate for us to find them and use them in this way.

JESUS' SELF-UNDERSTANDING

But what of the Messianic problem? Did Jesus claim to be Messiah? Did he possess a "Messianic consciousness"? Form criticism had eliminated the Messianic categories from the sayings of the historical Jesus on the ground that these categories reflect the faith of the post-Easter church. This elimination is still maintained by the post-Bultmannian scholars, and in fact, as we shall see, it is carried to even greater lengths by some of them. Of course, let us remind ourselves, this is not because these scholars do not personally believe in Jesus' Messiahship, or rather in what that mythological confession of faith stands for—they are not unbelievers, or even liberal Protestants who subtly modernize what is meant by Messiahship and eliminate the redemptive act of God. They are not trying to recover a simple Jesus who was just a teacher or a Jewish reformer. Their concern is simply to apply objectively a sound and relevant historical methodology. What then are the results? Bultmann, it will be remembered, allowed [26] some of the Son of man sayings to stand as authentic logia of Jesus, namely those which speak of the future work of the apocalyptic Son of man. But he held that Jesus did not identify himself with that Son of man, but looked for his coming as a figure quite distinct from himself, as Mark 8:38 and Luke 12:8f. (a saying testified both by Mark and Q) clearly show. There is an interesting divergence of opinion among the post-

[26] *Theology of the New Testament* I, p. 30.

Bultmannian scholars on this matter. Some of them (we might call them the right-wing school [27]) follow Bultmann in accepting as authentic those sayings about the coming Son of man which distinguish between Jesus and the Son of man. Since the post-Easter church came to identify Jesus with the coming Son of man, it is unthinkable for these scholars that the church should have created logia which make the distinction between them. This distinction is removed in the Son of man logia created by the post-Easter church. The sayings in question, however, speak of the coming Son of man, not as judge and redeemer, but as advocate (paraklete), and are wholly in line with Jesus' proclamation of the Reign of God as something which, though future, is presently operative in his word and work. A man's acceptance of Jesus and his message determines his acceptance or rejection at the coming of the kingdom of God. This distinction between Jesus and the coming Son of man corresponds to the distinction between the kingdom as it is breaking through in Jesus, and its final consummation. Now just as in the sayings about the kingdom Jesus' intention is not to impart teaching about the future kingdom, but to convey the decisiveness of the present moment of confrontation ("Blessed are you poor, for yours is (now) the (future) kingdom of God"), so Jesus, in speaking of the future Son of man, is not imparting teaching about that figure, but reinforcing the decisiveness of his own word and work for salvation. Heinz Tödt puts it in this way: while there is not a Christological identity between Jesus and the Son of man, there is a soteriological continuity between the work of the one and the work of the other. As a result of

[27] These include Günther Bornkamm, *Jesus of Nazareth*, p. 206, and H. E. Tödt, *The Son of Man in The Synoptic Tradition*, London, 1965 (German, 1959).

the Easter revelation the church came to see that Jesus was now identified with the coming Son of man, for God had vindicated Jesus and his eschatological message. Consequently, the church was able to carry the term "Son of man" as it were over to the other side of the equation, to Jesus in his earthly work. This happened very early, already in the oral tradition before it diverged into Q and Mark. Thus we get the sayings which speak of Jesus in his earthly work speaking of himself as Son of man. This, however, is not a mere self-designation: it expresses precisely that authority of Jesus which is apparent in the authentic sayings such as Mark 8:38, and which there is to be vindicated by the Son of man.

The "left wing" Bultmannians [28] take what at first sight appears to be a more radical line. They agree in eliminating from the authentic logia of Jesus not only those sayings which speak of the Son of man in his earthly work and in the passion, but even those which speak of him as coming at the End. Even these are, for them, creations of the post-Easter church, words of primitive Christian prophets. Conzelmann and Vielhauer are so impressed by the immediacy and finality of God's presence in Jesus that there can be no room for a second soteriological figure between Jesus and the coming Kingdom, as Bultmann and his right wing pupils had postulated. This is analogous to the more conservative positions of E. Schweizer and John A. T. Robinson,[29] who accept the sayings which identify Jesus in his earthly work

[28] E. Käsemann, "Sätze heiligen Rechtes im neuen Testament," *NTS*, 1, 4, 1954–55, pp. 248–260; Hans Conzelmann, *ZThK*, 54, 1957, p. 281, and art., "Jesus Christus," *RGG* (see p. 26); and Philipp Vielhauer, "Gottesreich und Menschensohn in der Verkündigung Jesu," in *Festschrift für Günther Dehn*, ed., W. Schneemelcher, 1957, pp. 51–79.

[29] E. Schweizer, *ZNW*, 50, 1959, pp. 185–209; John A. T. Robinson, *Jesus and His Coming*, London, 1957.

with the Son of man, and tend rather to eliminate the sayings which speak of the coming Son of man as post-Easter creations. Conzelmann then seeks to answer the problem why it is that the title Son of man is found only on the lips of Jesus, not as a confession of faith on the lips of others —an argument often used in favor of the authenticity of the Son of man logia. The reason for this, he says, is that in the early church Jesus was not *confessed* as Son of man, but *expected* to come as such. Thus the term Son of man is used only in creations of early Christian prophets, in which the exalted Jesus speaks as the coming Son of man, revealing himself as such to his expectant church. Vielhauer's attempt to eliminate even the future sayings is much more thorough-going. Following a line of argument which had already been put forward by an American scholar, H. B. Sharman,[30] Vielhauer points out that the Son of man sayings never speak of the kingdom of God, and conversely the kingdom of God sayings never speak of the Son of man. The two sets of logia therefore belong to different strata of the tradition. The question is, which of them goes back to Jesus? It is, argues Vielhauer, universally accepted that the kingdom of God was the central concept in the proclamation of Jesus. Therefore the kingdom of God logia must in general be accepted as authentic, and the Son of man sayings of all three types as creations of the post-Easter church. This is further substantiated by the fact that in the pre-Christian Jewish tradition also the combination of Son of man with kingdom of God is never found. It is true that the combination seems to appear in Dan. 7, but there, according to Vielhauer, the Son of man is not an individual redemptive figure, but a symbol for the saints of the Most High. In

[30] *Son of Man and Kingdom of God,* New York and London, 1944. Sharman's theological presuppositions, however, were those of an old-fashioned liberal.

Enoch the term, kingdom of God, never occurs, and in IV Ezra 13 the actual term, kingdom of God, is studiously avoided. In the Rabbinic tradition the term, kingdom of God, is never combined with the expectation of the Messiah,[31] nor conversely when they speak of the Messiah do the Rabbis mention the kingdom of God. Whereas the right wing Bultmannians postulate the resurrection encounters as the cause of the transference of the term Son of man from the coming One to Jesus in his earthly work, the left wing postulate it as the cause of the creation of all the Son of man logia. This forces Vielhauer to overlook the distinction between Jesus and the Son of man in such sayings as Mark 8:38. However, he concludes on a positive note. The resurrection revealed to the disciples that Jesus now lives in the glory of God. It therefore becomes necessary for them to insert Jesus' person into their proclamation of the kingdom of God, since with his death and resurrection the kingdom of God had now broken in. The early church therefore picked up the term, Son of man, in order to express the identity of the earthly Jesus with the exalted one. They had precedent for this in Enoch 71, where the man Enoch is exalted as Son of man. Vielhauer's essay concludes with words which are worth quoting:

> From this, the oldest faith in the Son of man, the sayings about the coming Son of man are derived. They objectivize a particular moment in the proclamation of Jesus by isolating it, and thus they introduce that concentration of the interest of faith in the person of Jesus which has left its deposit in the various christologies of the New Testament. Just as these christologies with all their variety and contra-

---

[31] As Tödt points out, *op. cit.,* p. 331, Vielhauer has slipped up here: if the Rabbis spoke of the *Son of man* rather than of the Anointed One, this observation would be pertinent. Since they do not, it has no bearing on Jesus' usage.

dictions point to the essentially provisional character of all christology, so does the starting-point of christology, the faith in the Son of man, point to their necessity. Yet the problem of christology cannot be solved by recourse to the so-called historical Jesus, any more than it can by taking refuge in the so-called historical, biblical Christ.[32]

AN IMPLICIT CHRISTOLOGY

Since this subject is so important, a few personal reactions would seem to be in place here. It is hard to believe that the church, if it had come as a result of the impact of the Easter revelation to identify Jesus with the coming Son of man as the expression of its faith, should either have coined such logia as Mark 8:38, Luke 12:8f. par., which expressly distinguish between Jesus and the coming Son of man (a point which, we have seen, Vielhauer conveniently ignores), or that it should have created Son of man sayings on such a wholesale scale had not Jesus himself used the term in authentic logia. In fact the rejection of Mark 8:38, Luke 12:8 par., as post-Easter creations offends against the primary criterion of tradition history, which is that sayings which conflict with the post-Easter faith of the church are *prima facie* authentic. They must therefore be retained as Jesuanic, and precisely in the sense that they distinguish between Jesus and the Son of man. But does this conflict with the insight derived from Jesus' eschatology, ethics and teaching about God, that they all imply a Christology? Does this insert another figure between Jesus and the coming kingdom? Far from it. Rightly understood, these sayings do not introduce the figure of the Son of man for his own sake, but precisely *for the sake of Jesus' own implicit christological self-under-*

[32] Vielhauer, *op. cit.,* p. 71.

standing. The Son of man merely acts as a kind of rubber stamp for the authority of Jesus' own word and person as the final eschatological self-communication of God. In calling men to fellowship with himself Jesus is giving them already here and now, by anticipation, the final salvation of the Kingdom of God. Once, however, the explicit identification of Jesus with the Son of man had been reached after Easter, the effect on Jesus' logia is a two-fold one. Sayings in which he had spoken simply as "I" now become sayings in which he speaks of himself as the Son of man. This has for instance clearly happened at Matt. 16:13 compared with Mark 8:27. It may equally have happened with at least some of the "present" Son of man sayings, e.g., Matt. 8:20 par. On the other hand, there was the opposite tendency to replace an original Son of man with "I," where Jesus had spoken of the Son of man, on the other side of the equation, the transcendental side, as a figure distinct from himself. This has clearly happened at Matt.10:32f. compared with Luke 12:8f.

THE DEATH OF JESUS

Günther Bornkamm's *Jesus of Nazareth* does not stop, as Bultmann's *Jesus and the Word* did, with the proclamation and teaching of Jesus, but goes significantly further. He includes a chapter on "Jesus and His Disciples," and another on his journey to Jerusalem, his passion and death, as essential and ascertainable parts of his history.[33] Though with Bultmann he regards Marcan predictions of the passion as *vaticinia ex eventu,* and creations of the post-Easter kerygmatic theology, and although like John Knox[34] he will not allow

[33] Cf. my criticism of Bultmann in *The Mission and Achievement of Jesus,* pp. 50f.

[34] *The Death of Christ,* New York, 1958, esp. Ch. III, "The Psychological Question."

that Jesus went up to Jerusalem deliberately to die (which would be tantamount to suicide), yet he thinks that the final journey to Jerusalem was deliberate. Its purpose was to confront Judaism at its very center with the challenge of his eschatological message. But with the fate of John the Baptist before him he could very well have known [35] that death was a possible, and indeed probable, outcome of this challenge. Bultmann in his only published (to 1960) reaction to the post-Bultmannian discussion [36] objects to this as psychological speculation: "It may be legitimate to say that Jesus' relationship to God presumed the passion right from the outset. But this ought not to be based on biographical and psychological considerations. All we ought to say is that Jesus' understanding of the will of God included the possibility that suffering might be necessary." However, Bornkamm's view is not entirely speculative, for it is based on Luke 13:31-33, which he regards as substantially authentic. Moreover, we do have one saying, which Bornkamm, like many other recent, highly critical writers [37] accept as authentic, and in which Jesus speaks of the meaning of his death (at a time when it was a certainty), explicitly relating that death to the coming of the kingdom of God. This is the eschatological prediction in the Supper narrative (Mark 14:25 par., Luke 22:16, 18). Unlike the other eucharistic sayings, this logion is above suspicion. It can hardly be a creation of the church's liturgical tradition, for as a matter

[35] Cf. E. Fuchs, *Studies,* p. 23; Knox, *op. cit.,* p. 120.

[36] "Allgemeine Wahrheit und christliche Verkündigung," in *Glauben und Verstehen* III, 1960, pp. 176f. Bultmann has since (1960) published a more extended reaction, E. tr. "The Christian Kerygma and the Historical Jesus" in *The Historical Jesus and the Kerygmatic Christ,* tr. and ed. C. E. Braaten and Roy A. Harrisville, New York and Nashville, 1964 (see Postscript to this chapter).

[37] E.g., E. Schweizer, art., "Abendmahl" in *RGG,* third ed.; Knox, *op. cit.,* p. 120.

of fact it was very early dropped from the liturgical for-
mula. In I Cor. 11:23–26 it survives in tenuous form in
the words, "until he comes," and in the early liturgies it
has completely disappeared. The eschatological prediction is of paramount importance and is the clue to Jesus'
interpretation of his death. In it Jesus declares that between him as he sat at supper and the coming of the Reign
of God there stood the decisive event of his death. Only
on the other side of it would he be re-united with his
disciples in the Messianic banquet. To that death he must
go alone, without them. But they will be restored to fellowship with him on the other side of that death when the
Reign of God comes. Of that reunion the Last Supper is
the pledge and promise.

THE CHURCH

On the question whether Jesus intended to found a church,
the Bultmann school see the church as the outcome of the
Easter event. Jesus envisaged only two things—the present
in which he was involved, and its vindication in the coming of
God's Reign. There was for him no room for an intervening
period between the present and the future. Also, the passage,
Matt. 16:18, while certainly Palestinian [38] is a creation of
the post-Easter church. But this is not the whole story. With
N. A. Dahl [39] one must say that insofar as the kingdom of
God, the end time, implies a people of God to enjoy it, the
notion of a reconstituted, eschatological community was implied as a part of Jesus' hope. The post-Bultmannians are
divided on the authenticity of the Twelve within the life-

---

[38] So even Bultmann, *The History of the Synoptic Tradition*, Oxford, 1963, pp. 138–140, and *Theology of the New Testament* I, p. 37.

[39] *Das Volk Gottes*, Oslo, 1941.

time of Jesus, but those who accept it would regard their number as a prophetic sign of the reconstitution of the people of God. But at the same time this qualification must be added: Jesus did not look for a continuing people of God in history, as the church turned out to be. He did not think in terms of an ecclesiastical organization, still less did he legislate for it. In that sense, the church is the end-result of his work, rather than his deliberate intention.

POSTSCRIPT:

BULTMANN ON THE POST-BULTMANNIANS

On July 25, 1959, Dr. Bultmann read a paper before the Heidelberger Akademie der Wissenschaften (see above, p. 44, footnote 36). This paper represents Bultmann's considered and detailed reaction to the post-Bultmannian resumption of the Quest of the Historical Jesus during the previous six years, and is therefore of great interest and importance.

He begins by recognizing that the new quest is by no means a resumption of the old one. Whereas the original quest was motivated by a desire to expose the difference between Jesus and the kerygma, the new quest seeks to demonstrate the historical continuity and the material relation (*sachliche Verhältnis*) between them. Bultmann thinks that in the discussion these two factors, historical continuity and material relation, have not been sufficiently distinguished. The establishment of the first factor is too often taken to imply the vindication of the second.

Having restated the palpable differences between Jesus and the kerygma, he turns to the first of these questions, the historical continuity. He defends himself against the charge

of denying this continuity, and agrees with the post-Bultmannian insistence that in the kerygma the risen Christ is
identical with the historical Jesus. The kerygma does not
mean any one other than the historical Jesus. He is careful
to say that the continuity is one between Jesus and the
kerygma, not between Jesus and the preached Christ: Jesus
and the kerygma being historical phenomena, there can be
a continuity between them, but since the risen Christ is not
a historical phenomenon, we cannot speak of a continuity
between the historical Jesus and the Christ of the kerygma.
It is the historical Jesus who is given a mythical interpretation in the kerygma: thus the kerygma presupposes the
historical Jesus. But—and this is the chief point which Bultmann refuses to concede to the post-Bultmannians—the
kerygma only presumes the bare facticity (the *Dass,* the
fact that he was), and is quite uninterested in the content
and character (the *Was* and the *Wie,* the "what" and "how")
of his history. He has a fairly easy task in demonstrating that
this is true of the Pauline and Johannine kerygma. Gal. 3:1
speaks of the cross, not as a biographical fact, but as a redemptive event. Phil. 2:6–8, Rom. 15:3 and II Cor. 8:9 speak
of the selflessness of Christ. But these passages are not speaking of the conduct of the earthly Jesus, but of the conduct
of the pre-existent figure. Here we are obliged to demur. We
agree that these affirmations are statements about the pre-
existent Christ. But if they are that and that only, they are
purely mythological statements tacked on to the mention of
the bare facticity of Jesus as though that were just a peg on
which to hang a myth. We would contend, however, that,
although made in mythological terms, they are not mere
mythology; they are made because of a *prior* encounter
with Jesus' history, because he had a history of a certain kind

and character. It is because of the selflessness, etc., of Jesus *in his history* that selflessness, etc., is predicated of the pre-existent "Son." That is why it is notoriously difficult to divide up Phil. 2:6–11 into neat phases, pre-existence, followed by incarnation and historical life. Does "emptied himself" refer only to the movement from pre-existence to incarnation, or does it refer also to the historical life of Jesus culminating in the cross? The answer is that it is speaking of the former, but is able to make that affirmation only because of what is seen in the latter. The same is true of the Johannine prologue: where does the evangelist cease to speak of the pre-existent Logos and move to the incarnate Logos? At verses 5, 9, 11, or 14? The answer again is, really at verse 14, but the evangelist is able to make these affirmations about the pre-existent Logos only because of the encounter with the Word made flesh.

To dispose of any concern with the content and character of Jesus' history and to confine it to the bare facticity is much more difficult for the synoptic kerygma, but Bultmann is not daunted. He admits that the gospels, against their direct intention, do disclose something of the character and content of Jesus' history. He examines the two attempts of contemporary, "past-historical" criticism (Jeremias, Althaus [40]) and of the modern existential-historical approach to rediscover more of the character and content of that history. Bultmann admits that the historico-critical attempt can discover a little about the historical Jesus.[41] But this does not

---

[40] J. Jeremias, "The Present Position in the Controversy Concerning the Problem of the Historical Jesus," *E.T.*, 59 (Aug., 1958), pp. 333–334; P. Althaus, *Fact and Faith in the Kerygma of Today*, tr., D. Cairns, Philadelphia, 1959 (British title: *The So-called Kerygma and the Historical Jesus*, Edinburgh and London, 1959), pp. 73f.

[41] It is interesting to see what Bultmann concedes: "With some degree of caution this much might be said about Jesus' activity: characteristic for him are exorcisms,

solve our greatest embarrassment, which is that we do not
know how Jesus interpreted his death. The various attempts
to escape from this embarrassment—Fuchs' "psychological"
explanation (see above, p. 44, n. 35), J. M. Robinson's existential explanation (*A New Quest,* p. 107) and Bornkamm's [42]
acceptance of the authenticity of Luke 13:31–33 and of the
eschatological prediction at the Last Supper—Bultmann finds
wholly unconvincing. All we know, he says, is that Jesus was
executed by the Romans as a political criminal. But what we
can reconstruct does not take us very far. So far from legiti-
mating the kerygma it only shows that the early church
had the opposite concern, to legitimate the *history* of Jesus
messianically. To this we should reply that in order to do just
this, the early church had to concern itself with more than
just the bare facticity of his history: the very fact that it
wrote the synoptic gospels shows that it was concerned with
the character and content of Jesus' history, however much
what it thought it knew about that history still remains
open to historical criticism. And not even Paul and John
are really exceptions to this as we have seen. Their interest
too extends beyond mere facticity.

The second attempt to relate Jesus to the kerygma which
Bultmann reviews is the attempt to show that in the word
and deed of Jesus the kerygma was already contained *in
nuce.* Here Bultmann goes some of the way with the post-
Bultmannians. He agrees that Jesus' own proclamation *im-*

---

the breach of the sabbath commandment, the infringement of the purity regula-
tions, polemic against Jewish legalism, association with the declassé such as
tax collectors and prostitutes, his friendliness towards women and children. We
can also see that Jesus was not an ascetic like John the Baptist; he enjoyed
food and drank a glass of wine. Perhaps too we may add that he called men
to discipleship and gathered around him a band of adherents, both men and
women." (p. 11)

[24] *Op. cit.,* pp. 154, 160 (see above, p. 26 and n. 2).

plies a Christology (Fuchs, Bornkamm, Conzelmann). And if Matt. 11:11–13, Luke 16:16 are authentic, Jesus interpreted his own appearance as the shift of the aeons.[43] This means that Jesus understood himself as an eschatological phenomenon. Bultmann also agrees with what Bornkamm [44] says about Jesus' *exousia* and the immediacy of the confrontation with God in him. But how far, Bultmann asks, does this take us? It only explains *how* the Proclaimer became the Proclaimed, but it does not mean that the kerygma is contained *in nuce* in Jesus' word and work. Otherwise the kerygma would simply have continued Jesus' proclamation. The kerygma, however, is essentially different: it proclaims him (we shall hear more of this later).

Bultmann then turns to the attempt to gain access to the historical Jesus by the existential approach to history. This approach attempts to demonstrate that there is a continuity, indeed an identity, between the self-understanding offered in Jesus and that offered in the kerygma. This attempt, however, poses an acute problem: *Why* (not *how,* we can demonstrate that, see above) did the Proclaimer become the Proclaimed? What was the inner necessity for that development? If the self-understanding offered in Jesus is identical with that offered in the kerygma, why did not the kerygma simply continue Jesus' proclamation? This problem, Bultmann notes, was clearly seen by the present writer in his review of James Robinson's book on the New Quest,[45] where he wrote: "The effort to demonstrate the continuity between Jesus and the kerygma may so blur the difference between

---

[43] See J. M. Robinson, *op. cit.,* p. 118.   [44] *Op. cit.,* pp. 53–63.

[45] See J. M. Robinson, *op. cit.,* pp. 120–125. Robinson has worked out this approach more methodically than any other post-Bultmannian. It also appears in H. Braun, Fuchs, Ebeling and Käsemann.

them, that in effect it will make the kerygma unnecessary." [46]
Bultmann's attempt to solve this problem is most significant,
and represents, for the present writer, the chief importance
of this paper. Neither the historico-critical approach nor
the existential-*geschichtlich* approach give us the same contact with Jesus as does the kerygma. For the contact with
Jesus which the kerygma gives us is neither merely *historisch*
nor even merely *geschichtlich:* it is *eschatological.* Through
the existential approach we can encounter Jesus and other
historical figures only as unique figures (*einmal*), who offer
us possibilities, among others, of self-understanding. In the kerygma, and only in the kerygma, we encounter One who was
not only unique (*einmal*) like other historical figures, but
once and for all (ein für allemal), One who confronts us
with an eschatological final, absolute claim, who offers the
final, authentic self-understanding. Less cautiously Bultmann adds that the Jesus whom we encounter by the historical approach is one who only *promised* salvation,[47]
whereas in the kerygma we encounter him as one who has
brought salvation and is now mediating it in the kerygma.
This, we maintain, is incautious. For, if, as Bultmann recognizes, the shift of the aeons in Jesus' perspective had already occurred in his own appearance (see above) then,
without lapsing into realized eschatology, we must say that
already in his historical appearance Jesus' proclamation
mediates a proleptic participation in and not merely a promise of the eschatological salvation: "Blessed are ye poor for

---

[46] *ATR,* 41 (1959), pp. 232–235. Bultmann adds in a footnote that two American
scholars, Erwin M. Good and Van A. Harvey, have voiced similar objections
in letters to him.

[47] Cf. *Glauben und Verstehen* I, Tübingen, 1933, p. 201. Jesus belonged to the
old era of the law, Paul to the new era of the gospel (J. M. Robinson, *op. cit.,*
p. 119).

yours is (now) the (future) kingdom of God." This is why, in the last analysis, it is *theologically* unsatisfactory to include Jesus as Bultmann does in his *Primitive Christianity*[48] in the section on "Judaism." Bultmann defends this procedure elsewhere in this paper (Jesus was a Jew, not a Christian).[49] But his defense covers only its *historical* (*historisch*) legitimacy. Bultmann again quotes the present writer with approval in this connection: "If . . . Easter discloses the achievement of a further phase of God's eschatological action, viz., that the Cross has inaugurated a greater degree of the 'already,' then the kerygma can mediate an encounter which the modern view of history cannot."[50] What Bultmann has not seen is that I have phrased more carefully my statement than he has framed his: "*a greater degree* of the already." Thus I recognize that there is some degree of the "already" in the historical Jesus; yet justice is done to the difference between this and the post-Easter situation in the kerygma. Or, to put it another way, as in *The Book of the Acts of God:* "The earliest church proclaimed that God had acted directly and decisively in Jesus. Jesus also had a proclamation. But it was understandably different from that of the earliest Church. He proclaimed, not that God *had* acted decisively, but that he was *in the process of acting* and was *about* to act decisively."[51] Here we would add that for Jesus it was precisely in him (Jesus) that God was beginning his eschatological act, just as for the post-Easter church in its kerygma it was precisely in Jesus that God had acted. It is this "in Jesus" that provides the implicit Christology of his own proclamation and the explicit

[48] *Primitive Christianity in Its Contemporary Setting,* tr., R. H. Fuller, London and New York, 1956, pp. 86–93.

[49] P. 8.   [50] *Ibid.,* p. 234.

[51] G. Ernest Wright and Reginald H. Fuller, Garden City, 1957, p. 240.

Christology of the kerygma. For Christology means Jesus as the vehicle of God's eschatological action. Thus we do justice both to the continuity and the difference between Jesus and kerygma. It is not merely a formal discontinuity and a material identity, as the post-Bultmannians present it, nor is it a material discontinuity (promise and fulfilment) as Bultmann himself presents it. The kerygma presents us not merely with the historical Jesus who is in the process of accomplishing his work. It presents us with a risen Christ who has accomplished his earthly work.

IV

Pauline Studies

As WE HAVE already had occasion to notice (see above, p. 31), the major part of Bultmann's *Theology of the New Testament* I is devoted to the theology of St. Paul. In a review John A. T. Robinson (now Bishop of Woolwich) remarked that this work gets better and better as it goes on, and is superb in its presentation of Pauline theology. This judgment has been widely shared. The key concept around which Bultmann expounds Pauline thought is its anthropology, its doctrine of man. Of course, this approach is naturally congenial to an existentialist interpretation, but it is also justified by the content of Paul's thought, especially in Romans.

BULTMANN ON PAUL

Bultmann divides his treatment of Paul into two main sections: Man prior to faith, and Man under faith. Under the first section he expounds Paul's psychological terms: *soma* (body), *psyche* (soul), *pneuma* (spirit), *zoe* (life); then mind, conscience and heart; flesh, sin and the world; and finally the law. His observations are pertinent and profound. But when he comes to Man under faith, Bultmann is compelled to modify his exclusively anthropological approach in order to deal with the "salvation occurrence" (*das Heilsereignis,* which would be better translated, "the redemptive event") and its extension through the word and sacraments in the church. Yet even in these later sections, the anthropological twist is evident. It is characteristic that the redemptive event is not confined to A.D. 1–30, but includes also the word of preaching in which it is made present.

The anthropological treatment of Paul is by no means new. It goes back to F. C. Baur of the famous Tübingen school,[1] and was continued by the modified Tübingen school, Pfleiderer, Weinel, etc. But they all interpreted Pauline anthropology in terms of Greek idealism. The "flesh," for instance, was equated with man's lower nature, the "spirit" with his "higher" nature. It is Bultmann's great merit that he has broken forever with this misunderstanding. These terms, he insists, must be interpreted not idealistically, but existentially. They speak not about parts of man, but of the whole man in his various possible relations with his "historical" environment, i.e., with wills and powers outside himself. Thus the antithesis between flesh and spirit is not one between the lower and higher natures: they describe

[1] See his *Paul, His Life and Work,* second ed., 1876 (first German ed., 1845).

not parts of man, but relationships. Flesh denotes man's bondage to the powers of evil, *pneuma* or spirit his life in faith. There is, however, even after faith, still a "not yet." Man is still subject to temptation. Authentic existence is not an assured possession, but has constantly to be renewed in faith and obedience. The indicative implies an imperative: "Become what you are." The sacraments, too, are not mystical rites of consecration, but the translation of man from the old existence to the new.

KÄSEMANN'S CRITICISMS

All this is very helpful and full of insight. It does much more justice to the Hebraic element in Paul's anthropology than did the older idealistic interpretation. Incidentally, it also brings Paul closer to modern views of man, whether psychological or existentialist. Nevertheless, this is not the whole story. And it is significant that some of the most pertinent criticisms of Bultmann's treatment of Paul come from members of the Bultmann school. For instance, in an article on present-day New Testament studies [2] Ernst Käsemann complains that Bultmann has reduced Paul's theology exclusively to an anthropology, whereas anthropology is only a part of it. Nor is it the primary part, for it is subordinated both to theology (the understanding of God) and to Christology (the understanding of man). With this criticism we might compare Karl Barth's frequent insistence —of which his treatment of the doctrine of man in *Kirchliche Dogmatik* III/2 is a monument—that all anthropology must start from the Man Christ Jesus, i.e., its center must be the work of God in Christ, which is prior to any specif-

[2] "Neutestamentliche Fragen von heute," *ZThK*, 54, 1957, pp. 1–21, esp. pp. 12–15.

ically Christian understanding of man. Anthropology in the Christian sense is the understanding of man which proceeds from the Christ event. The Christ event must not be absorbed into an anthropology and made simply a part of it. Käsemann's second criticism is that while this insistence on an anthropological interpretation of Paul certainly has the merit of preventing the dissolution of the proclamation of Christ into a myth (in the sense of "unrelated to human existence") the result is an excessively individualistic understanding of the content of salvation. It ignores the context of redemptive history [3] in which Paul places his theology, and the corporate and cosmological dimensions of his thought. These are substantially the same criticisms which have been passed above on Bultmann's demythologizing as a whole. This is more than a coincidence, for Bultmann tends to reduce Paul (and John [4]) to good disciples of the Bultmann school!

DAHL'S CRITICISMS

A further significant reaction to Bultmann's presentation of Pauline theology is to be found in an extensive review of his book by N. A. Dahl,[5] a Norwegian New Testament scholar of international fame who studied under Bultmann. Dahl points out first that the general structure of Bultmann's presentation—"Man prior to faith" and "Man under faith"—is justified by the structure of Romans 1–11, corresponding respectively to chapters 1–3 and chapters 4–11.

---

[3] With this compare the present writer's remarks in *The Book of the Acts of God*, G. Ernest Wright and Reginald H. Fuller, Garden City, 1957, pp. 288ff.

[4] Cf. the review of Bultmann's *Theology of the New Testament* II by the present writer in *The Living Church*, May 5, 1959, pp. 19–20.

[5] *TR*, n.f. 22, 1954, pp. 21–40.

It is also suggested by the Pauline pattern of exhortation:
"Ye were sometime . . . but now are ye"; "Put off the old
man . . . put on the new man."

Dahl also points out that it is only fair to note that Bultmann separates Paul's kerygmatic presuppositions from the
main treatment of his theology and places them in the
previous chapter on "The Kerygma of the Hellenistic
Church." This must be remembered in judging the apparently unbalanced anthropological treatment of Paul in
the chapter on his theology. This procedure has certain ad-
vantages. It shows that Paul was not so much of an innovator
as it used to be supposed in the days before the rise of the
History of Religions School, and particularly by Bousset.
After all, Paul had much in common with general apostolic
Christianity, especially on its Hellenistic side. The arrangement also enables the distinctive contributions of Paul to
stand out more clearly by themselves.

But Dahl also has some criticisms. Like Käsemann, he
complains that Bultmann's approach is too exclusively anthropological. God and his being are prior to man and *his*
being, and of God and his being little account is taken. This
explains why Bultmann has so little to say about the Old
Testament in connection with Paul's thought. A new and
important point of criticism is that Bultmann neglects Romans 9-11, in which the Pauline doctrine of justification,
as expounded in the earlier chapters, is set in the wider context and framework of redemptive history (*Heilsgeschichte*).
This reminds us of Johannes Munck's thesis in *Paul and
the Salvation of Mankind*,[6] which provides an important
corrective to Bultmann at this point. Far from being a
peripheral digression, Rom. 9-11, Dahl maintains, is really

[6] London and Richmond, 1959. E. tr. of *Paulus und die Heilsgeschichte*, Aarhus,
1954. This book will be discussed at length below.

the central clue to and the basis for the Pauline doctrine of justification. This is just one example of Bultmann's "unhistorical" treatment of Paul: "One may ask whether this 'dehistoricizing' of the New Testament is not really more characteristic of Bultmann's theology than his famous program of demythologizing." And again: "Here we may ask whether Bultmann does not so absolutize his philosophical (i.e., existentialist) presuppositions that he decides already beforehand what the New Testament is allowed to say and what it is not allowed to say"—which is a similar criticism to Käsemann's charge that Bultmann makes Paul a good disciple of Rudolf Bultmann. By "unhistorical" Dahl means, locating the redemptive work of God exclusively in the existence of the individual and leaving little to be said about the people of God as an on-going factor within (though not of) history.

Dahl next turns to discuss Bultmann's treatment of the Pauline doctrine of the cross and resurrection. Here the relation between the redemptive event and believing self-understanding stands out most clearly. Grace is characterized as event. So far, so good. But what event? Bultmann begins by elucidating the various images under which Paul expounds the cross: redemption, victory, sacrifice, concepts derived either from Jewish or Gnostic mythology. All of these images, however, are, Bultmann asserts, problematical, for they all convey the impression that before we can accept the kerygma as addressed to us personally in our concrete situation we have to accept certain historical and mythological propositions as true. We must believe that Jesus did die, that his death was redemption, victory, and sacrifice. We must believe that he was the pre-existent Son of God who became incarnate. But these are only mythological propositions for what takes place in the preaching of the word as address, as God's action for me (*pro me*): "The salvation event is *nowhere present* except in the proclaiming, accosting, demanding and promising word of preaching." [7] The little word "nowhere," italicized by the present writer, would seem to justify the quip alluded to earlier that for the theology of demythologizing the redemptive event occurs not on the first Good Friday, but when Dr. Bultmann ascends the pulpit at 11 a.m. on a Sunday morning. And it also seems to justify the quip emanating from Germany that for Bultmann Jesus ascended not into heaven but into the kerygma. And it gives point to the story (which may be apocryphal, though it is certainly "mythologically" true!) that once when Bultmann had a birthday his students presented him with a demythologized Bible, a massive tome which was found to contain only one word—KERYGMA! Now while this may be true of Bultmann's own theological position, is it equally true of Paul? Bultmann himself is, perhaps a little uncomfortably, aware that it is not quite. But he hastens to add that this is what Paul meant or ought to have said: it "corresponds to his intention."

Now, Dahl continues, Bultmann is quite right in insisting that the kerygma is address. It is perfectly true that *we* encounter the redemptive event only in the preaching (including the sacraments). The preaching is certainly *part* of the redemptive event. It is equally true that to regard the kerygma as the impartation of objective facts or the purveyance of information is a falsification of faith. The kerygma is not an objective piece of knowledge to be bandied about and discussed outside of our acceptance of it as *pro nobis*. Yet the kerygma does report facts, both historical and "mythological," at least so far as Paul himself is concerned.

The redemptive event has happened before our decision

[7] *Theology of the New Testament* I, p. 302.

(and, one should add, before it is preached). It does not become redemptive only when it is preached and believed. True, God is not encountered outside of the word and faith —but this does not mean that he has no existence outside of the word and faith. False objectifying occurs only when the redemptive event is rationalized, as in a scholastic theory of the atonement, or when the witness to the resurrection is taken as objective proof. It is in the word and sacraments that the prior mythological event is made present to us.[8]

We might add that there is latent in Bultmann's thinking a kind of unitarianism of the third person. If, unmythologically speaking, "Holy Spirit" means the redemptive event as a present reality in the church's kerygma, God encountering us in the word responded to in faith, God *pro nobis,* it needs to be complemented by a doctrine of the "second person," which, demythologized, means God going out in revealing and redeeming activity in his word, made flesh in the event of A.D. 1–30. The kerygma is the *extension* of this event, not the event itself in and of itself. In the undemythologized language of the New Testament, the Spirit does not speak on his own authority, but testifies of Christ: "He will take of mine and declare it to you" (John 16:14). "The Spirit had not yet been given, because Jesus had not yet been glorified" (John 7:39). If there is to be a kerygma at all, if there is to be "Spirit," there must be the prior decisive event. God in the kerygma is God acting *pro me.* God in the Christ event is God acting *pro se.* And the God who is there acting *pro se* is the God who is the Creator of the world and who is prior to his act of creation. While it is true that we cannot know God as he is in himself, but only in his self-disclosure through his acts of creation, redemption and sanctification, yet the God who so discloses

[8] See Dahl, *TR, op. cit.,* p. 43.

himself is the God who exists prior to those self-disclosures. It is not therefore the intrusion of a non-biblical, Greek ontology when we speak of God's prior being. The Old Testament does so too—precisely on the ground of God's self-disclosure in his mighty acts:

> Before the mountains were brought forth,
> or ever thou hadst formed the earth and the world,
> from everlasting to everlasting thou art God
>
> (Ps. 90:2)

Is this mythology because it is not existential—i.e., a statement about my own existence? Or is it a genuine insight proceeding from the faith encounter? So the biblical proclamation implies an affirmation about the prior being of God, an affirmation about God in himself and God for himself, as well as about God for us. In the (mythological) New Testament triad, God is therefore "Father, Son and Holy Spirit." [9]

To resume Dahl's review of the *Theology of the New Testament,* the final point he makes—and it is in similar vein to the foregoing—he complains that Bultmann reduces Jesus to a cipher, an event which really occurs in preaching and in faith.

In a concluding summary, Dahl agrees that certain elements in Pauline thought receive correct emphasis. But others have been neglected. The redemptive, objective aspect is missing, and the place of the distinctively Pauline elements in the New Testament as a whole is misconstrued. These elements represent a deepening and corrective to the general apostolic kerygma, not a demythologized substitute for it.

---

[9] For a more extended discussion of the "historical" interpretation of the doctrine of the Trinity, cf. the article by the present writer, "On Demythologizing the Trinity," in *ATR,* 43, No. 2, April, 1961, pp. 121–131.

When these elements are made the criterion for the New Testament proclamation as a whole they lead to a one-sided, ultra-Paulinism. Shades of Marcion—the ever-present temptation of Lutheranism!

MUNCK ON PAUL

Another important contribution to Pauline studies was published in German by the Danish scholar, Johannes Munck (see above, p. 58, n. 6). Unlike Bultmann, whose discussion of Paul's theology has a curiously abstract, timeless quality, Munck insists that Paul's writing has to be seen in terms of the concrete situation in which it was written. His letters are part of his missionary activity just as the tennis racket is an extension of the human hand. That activity was motivated by a distinctive concept of redemptive history (*Heilsgeschichte*). Jewish apocalyptic hoped for the entry of Israel first at the *parousia,* after which such Gentiles (if any) who belonged to the elect, would be admitted.[10]

Jesus himself and the earliest church apparently accepted this order of expectation, and the mission to Israel was conducted by the Jerusalem church on this assumption. The Gentiles, while not excluded in principle from the salvation in Christ, could wait until after the *parousia.* Since, however, the policy of the Jerusalem church had patently failed with the rejection of the gospel by the majority of Israel, it was given to Paul to reverse the order of events and revise the church's missionary policy accordingly. Now the order was to be: Gentiles, Israel, *parousia.* This was not a thought-out decision of the apostle, but a *mysterion* communicated to him, as expounded in Rom. 9–11. Here, in fact, was the

[10] Cf. J. Jeremias, *Jesus' Promise to the Nations,* London and Naperville, 1958, *passim.*

only serious theological difference between Paul and the Jerusalem church. This was the point at issue at the so-called apostolic council at Jerusalem as related in Gal. 2:1–10. Here the so-called "gentleman's agreement" was reached, a compromise solution under which Peter and Paul were to head two missions, the Jews and Gentiles respectively. Each mission was based on a different conception of redemptive history.

Paul therefore conceives it to be his mission to play the decisive role in phase one of redemptive history, i.e., the bringing in of the Gentiles. The result of this, he hopes, will be that Israel will be "provoked to jealousy," so that phase two will follow, namely the gathering in of Israel. To accelerate the process Paul hastens to spread the gospel in the Gentile world, planting the church at representative centers in the Roman Empire. This idea of representation must be understood in its full seriousness. It is not that Paul opens a mission at strategic centers in the hope that the surrounding country will be evangelized from those centers. That would be altogether too modern an interpretation of Paul's procedure. Rather, he was gathering from all the provinces of the Roman Empire a nucleus, representing the gathering in of the "fullness of the Gentiles." In the execution of this plan Paul attaches signal importance to the collection from the Gentile churches for the church at Jerusalem. This, contends Munck, was more than a charitable act of relief, more too than a symbol of the unity between the two halves of the church, Jew and Gentile. It was a demonstration that the fullness of the Gentiles was now being gathered in, contrary to Jewish expectation (see above). Seeing this demonstration, Israel would be provoked to jealousy, and want to come in too. This reconstruction is based on an exegesis of II Thess. 2:6–7, and more particularly of Rom. 9–11, to which Munck has since devoted an entire monograph. We have already seen how Bultmann practically neglected these chapters in his treatment of Pauline thought.[11]

PAUL'S OPPONENTS

Munck's thesis, which we have outlined above, actually occupies only a small part of his book (68 pages in the English translation, out of a total of 334 pages). The rest of the book is an extended refutation of the still widespread notion, dating back to F. C. Baur (see above, p. 55), that there was a sharp antithesis in the early church between Paul on the one hand and the Jerusalem apostles on the other. While it is commonly taken for granted that such scholars as J. B. Lightfoot in England and Theodore Zahn in Germany demolished the Tübingen hypothesis, all that they actually destroyed was the chronology of the Tübingen school. In other words, the dialectical process of Jewish Christianity, Paulinism and the synthesis in early catholicism was accomplished by the end of the first century instead of stretching into the second. Of course, the original Tübingen classification of the various New Testament writings as thesis, antithesis and synthesis literature has also been modified. Yet most of our standard guides to the study of St. Paul—Dibelius, Lietzmann, A. D. Nock and W. L. Knox, for instance—are, we are surprised to learn, still committed

---

[11] It is true that in an article entitled "The Transformation of the Idea of the Church in the History of Early Christianity" in *The Canadian Journal of Theology*, 1, 1955, pp. 73–81, Bultmann pays more attention to *Heilsgeschichte* and its place in Pauline thought, especially in Rom. 9–11. But characteristically he resorts to criticism: this emphasis on *Heilsgeschichte* represents an "inconsistency" in Paul's otherwise existential understanding of history. Therefore in the end it is eliminated even here. For another treatment of Pauline theology in terms of *Heilsgeschichte*, see C. K. Barrett, *From First Adam to Last*, New York, 1962.

basically to the Tübingen view. The ghost of Baur is far from dead! It is still widely assumed that there was a basic disagreement if not between Peter and Paul, then certainly between Paul and James the brother of the Lord; and that Judaizing emissaries from James dogged Paul's steps at every turn and wrought havoc in all his churches.

Munck therefore undertakes an extended refutation of the exegesis on which this view rests. It is relevant to his primary thesis insofar as he had argued that the sole point at issue between Paul and the Jerusalem apostolate was their respective understanding of redemptive history. The Judaizers in the Galatian churches were not emissaries from James, but local trouble-makers. It is a common, but quite unwarranted, assumption that these disturbers of the peace in Galatia were identical with the "certain men from James" mentioned in Gal. 2:12, who had caused trouble in Antioch at an earlier date over the quite different issue of the common meals in that church at which Jew and Gentile sat at meat together. Again, it is commonly held that there were various parties in the church at Corinth, one of which was a Judaizing party under orders from James (Baur had identified it with the "Christ party" of I Cor. 1:12). Munck undertakes to show that there were really no "parties" at Corinth at all, at least not in any doctrinal sense. Rather, they were simply cliques who imagined that the gospel was just another version of Hellenistic wisdom. These cliques had quite gratuitously attached themselves to Apollos, Paul, Peter, etc., as convenient labels, largely from motives of snobbery. The "false apostles" of II Cor. 11:12ff. did not emanate from Jerusalem—that is nowhere stated—nor did they hold to any particular doctrinal line. They were simply unauthorized persons of uncertain origin who sponged on the Corinthians after Paul's settlement with them and so jeopardized the collection for the saints at Jerusalem. Munck, incidentally, like many Continental scholars, rejects the partition theories of II Corinthians, and therefore holds that II Cor. 10–13 was written *after* chapters 1–9. Nor is there any evidence that there were Judaizers at Rome when Paul wrote Romans. Here Munck follows the brilliant thesis of T. W. Manson.[12] According to this Romans was written as a circular letter to all of the Pauline churches as a summary of the position he had reached in the controversies in Galatia and Corinth, a copy of it in a special edition being sent also to Rome as a self-introduction to a church which Paul had not yet visited. Consequently Romans cannot be used as evidence for the situation in the Christian community in Rome. Finally, Munck follows Lohmeyer in identifying the opponents of Phil. 3:2ff. not with Judaizers, but with Jews. Not all of Munck's interpretations are convincing, though the present writer would now admit that there is perhaps more to be said in favor of them than he thought at the time when he reviewed the German edition of the book.[13]

There is indeed much to be said for the view that Galatians was directed against local trouble-makers. In fact, it is becoming increasingly probable that they were not Judaizers in the proper sense of the word at all, but rather represented a gnosticizing movement with Jewish affinities. The allusion to their calendrical observances (Gal. 4:10) seems to support this.[14]

A good deal of attention has in fact been devoted in recent years to the identity of Paul's opponents. We have

[12] "St. Paul's Letter to the Romans—and Others," *BJRL*, 31, 1948, pp. 224-240.
[13] In *JTS*, n.s. 6/2, 1955, pp. 284-287.
[14] See the article, "The Anomaly of Galatians," by Chalmer E. Faw in *BR*, 4, 1960, pp. 25-38.

already seen Munck's attempt to give the *coup de grace* to Baur's theory that Paul's opponents everywhere were the Judaizers whom he identified with the original Jerusalem apostolate. In a striking series of essays one of Bultmann's pupils, Walter Schmithals, has studied the major Pauline epistles and propounded the thesis that while Baur was right in attributing the opposition to Paul everywhere to the same party, Paul's opponents were Jewish-Christian gnostics, who had nothing whatever to do with the Jerusalem apostolate.[15] Schmithals infers that there was one single group of Jewish-Christian gnostic propagandists who dogged Paul's steps from church to church, very much as Baur supposed his Judaizers had done. A more discriminating position is taken by H. Köster and G. Bornkamm: while the opponents everywhere are gnostics, they represent varying tendencies, some more Jewish, others more Hellenistic.[16]

PARTITION THEORIES

The consideration of the opposition of Paul has led further to a revival and extended application of partition theories to the Pauline epistles. English-speaking readers have long been familiar with the partition of II Cor. 10–13 and II Cor. 1–9, for it has become very widely accepted by British and American scholars;[17] it has long been out of vogue in

[15] W. Schmithals, *Die Gnosis in Korinth,* Göttingen, 1956; *Paulus und die Gnosis,* Hamburg, 1965.

[16] H. Köster, "Häretiker im Urchristentum," *RGG,* third ed., III, 1958, cols. 17–21; G. Bornkamm, "Die Vorgeschichte des sogenannten Zweiten Korintherbriefes," *Sitzungsberichte des Heidelberger Akademie der Wissenschaften,* Phil.-hist. Klasse, 1961, p. 17.

[17] E.g., R. H. Strachan, *The Second Epistle of Paul to the Corinthians* (Moffatt

Germany, where it first originated (Hausrath, 1870).[18] Paul is supposed either to have had a sleepless night or received fresh news between the writing of II Cor. 9 and 10! Now Hausrath's theory has not only been revived but extended. Schmithals and Bornkamm (see footnotes 15 and 16 above, p. 68) find no less than four or five letters or fragments of letters in II Cor., while the former scholar divides I Cor. into two letters and Phil. into three. K. G. Eckart[19] divides I Thess. into three. Not all of these proposals are equally convincing, but Bornkamm has put up a good case for his views on II Cor. and Schmithals for Phil.[20] Bornkamm has also broken new ground by asking why the Pauline epistles have been arranged as they have been, and finds in their arrangement important clues to the theology of the sub-apostolic age, an important parallel to the new interest in the composition of the evangelists as a clue to their theology.

Commentary), London, 1935; A. D. Nock, *St. Paul*, London and New York, 1938, pp. 172f.; T. W. Manson, "St. Paul in Ephesus, (3) The Corinthian Correspondence," *BJRL*, 19, 1941–42 (shortly to be republished in a collected series of essays by Manchester University Press).

[18] E.g., H. Lietzmann–W. G. Kümmel, *An die Korinther*, Handbuch zum Neuen Testament, 9th ed., 1950, pp. 139f.; Munck, *op. cit.*, pp. 168–171.

[19] "Der zweite echte Brief des Apostels Paulus an die Thessalonicher," *ZThK*, 58, 1961, pp. 30–44.

[20] See also F. W. Beare, *A Commentary on the Epistle to the Philippians*, London and New York, 1959, pp. 24–29.

V

Synoptic Studies

THAT THE SYNOPTIC GOSPELS consist of four main strata is one of the accepted conclusions of form criticism. The lowest layer consists of Jesus' *ipsissima verba* and authentic memories of his deeds substantially uncolored by the Easter experiences of the earliest church. It was with this layer that we were concerned in Chapter III. Next comes the layer consisting of the contribution of the earliest post-Easter Palestinian community—the transformation of its memories of Jesus' words and deeds in the light of the Easter faith: its modifications and additions to the traditions of Jesus' words and deeds. Then comes the contribution of the Hellenistic churches. They translated the Aramaic traditions from the Palestinian churches into Greek, and added to them new sayings which they erroneously attributed to Jesus. These additions, like those of the Palestinian communities, were made in good faith. Partly they were circulated as revelations to Christian prophets from the risen Lord (cf. the utterances of the risen Christ in the Apocalypse). Partly too they arose from the need to reapply the traditions of Jesus' teachings to new situations in the church. The uppermost layer consists of the contribution of the evangelists themselves. Now of these four strata the second and third, namely the anonymous contributions of the Palestinian and Hellenistic churches in the oral stage, were the main preoccupation of the form critics. Occasionally, as in the two Jesus-books of Bultmann and Dibelius, some attention was paid to the earliest stratum, the words of Jesus. But in the main, with the partial exception of Karl Ludwig Schmidt's study of the Marcan framework and of some of Dibelius' essays now published in a collected volume [1] there was at that time very little interest in the contributions of the evangelists for their own sake. There was a tendency to regard the evangelists as little more than collectors of oral traditions. The evangelists stood as it were at the end of a pipeline: they collected in a bucket what came through, and arranged it a little, but exhibited no real creativity of their own, and made very little personal contribution to New Testament theology. The present writer remembers that eccentric Jewish scholar, Robert Eisler, remarking in a conversation at Oxford in 1940 that he did not like the form critics because they were "socialists"—they thought the gospels were the anonymous products of the communities—and Eisler for his part was a rugged individualist!

---

[1] *Botschaft und Geschichte* I, Tübingen, 1953, esp. the essay, "Evangelienkritik und Christologie," pp. 293–358, which originally appeared in English as *Gospel Criticism and Christology*, London, 1935.

Recent study of the gospels has tended toward a greater appreciation of the evangelists as creative theologians in their own right; each offers his distinctive interpretation of the traditions with which he worked. This new realization, incidentally, is the latest of a whole series of developments in the past thirty years which has diminished the formerly wide gap between the synoptics and the fourth gospel. The differences between them are still there, and they are very great. But both the synoptists and John use oral traditions, arranging them freely for their own kerygmatic purposes. The main difference is that the synoptists have to work with more modest means. If we are to study the work of the evangelists themselves, we must pay very close attention to their editorial redactions—the connecting links they forge between the pericopes, their arrangement of the pericopes, the alterations they make to their sources where we have them. It is easy to see how Matthew and Luke altered Mark, and by comparison and inference we can form some idea of their alterations of the Q material, though in the nature of the case these remain more conjectural. Also their selection and omission of material is significant. A number of studies along these lines have appeared in recent years, most, but not all, of them from the Bultmann school. For Mark we have W. Marxsen's *Der Evangelist Markus*[2] and James M. Robinson's *The Problem of History in Mark*.[3] On Luke we have Hans Conzelmann's *The Theology of St. Luke*.[4] For

[2] Göttingen, 1956 (second ed., 1959).

[3] London and Naperville, 1957. First published in German under the more descriptive title, *Das Geschichtsverständnis des Markusevangeliums*, Zurich, 1956.

[4] London and New York, 1960 (second ed.). First published in German under the title of *Die Mitte der Zeit*. The German title, as we shall see, defines more succinctly the author's thesis.

Matthew we have an essay by Günther Bornkamm published in the Dodd *Festschrift*[5] and a collection of essays by Bornkamm and two of his pupils.[6] Finally there is Bornkamm's article on the gospels, s.v. "Evangelien," in the third edition of *Religion in Geschichte und Gegenwart*.

CRITICAL PRESUPPOSITIONS

First, let us review the standpoint of these authors on the source criticism of the gospels, a matter which plays an important part in the kind of questions they are raising. The two-source theory (priority of Mark and the Q hypothesis) still stands, despite recent attacks on it from various quarters: Vaganay and Butler among Roman Catholic scholars,[7] Schlatter and his pupils in the 1930's at Tübingen,[8] the American Anglican scholar Pierson Parker,[9] all of which seek to reassert the priority of Matthew, and the rather cavalier

[5] "Enderwartung und Kirche im Matthäusevangelium" (see above, p. 2, n. 3), pp. 222–260. Also printed in the work next mentioned (n. 6.).

[6] G. Bornkamm, G. Barth and H. J. Held, *Tradition and Interpretation in Matthew*, London, 1963 (German, 1960). The reader will find some references to this volume in E. P. Blair's *Jesus in the Gospel of Matthew*, New York, 1960: Chapter I of this work is a very useful summary of recent studies of St. Matthew's gospel.

[7] L. Vaganay, *Le Problème synoptique*, Paris, 1954; B. C. Butler, *The Originality of St. Matthew*, Cambridge, 1951. For a detailed and, in its cumulative effect, convincing refutation of Butler's arguments, see the forthcoming work, C. F. D. Moule, *The Birth of the New Testament*, London and New York, Excursus IV, "The Priority of Mark," by G. M. Styler.

[8] Schlatter, who died at an advanced age in 1938, was the moving spirit behind the *Theologisches Wörterbuch zum Neuen Testament*. He upheld the priority of Matt. and rejected the Q hypothesis. Even Gerhard Kittel, the editor of the *Wörterbuch* in its earlier stage, believed that Schlatter had successfully demolished the Q hypothesis though not the priority of Mark.

[9] *The Gospel Before Mark*, Chicago, 1953.

views of Austin Farrer.[10] The latter, while still maintaining the priority of Mark, thinks that the facts which led to the Q hypothesis can be more simply accounted for if we suppose that Matthew used Mark, while Luke in turn used both Matthew and Mark. Simple and attractive though this last theory is, it is open to a fatal objection. Matthew has tidily collected the Q material into great blocks. Luke, we must then suppose, has broken up this tidy arrangement and scattered the Q material without rhyme or reason all over his gospel—a case of unscrambling the egg with a vengeance! Most of us, the post-Bultmannians included, still accept the priority of Mark. We are a little less sure of the Q hypothesis, at least in its rigid form. It is best to regard it with E. Fascher as a "layer of tradition" rather than as a single document. This tradition of the sayings of Jesus was in state of fluidity, and available to Matthew and Luke in different forms. All three synoptic writers, according to Bornkamm,[11] had special traditions of their own, Mark included. Here we have shades of the Ur-Markus theory, which has always had greater vogue in Germany than in the English speaking world, where it is assumed, perhaps a little too easily, that B. H. Streeter buried it for good and all. Mark, it is thought by the Bultmann scholars, was not available to Matthew and Luke in quite the same form, not yet in the form in which it was more or less finally standardized in the canon.

[10] "On Dispensing with Q," in *Studies in the Gospels* (see above, p. 29, n. 11). It is hard to think that the patient work over many years by members of his own university, Sir John Hawkins (*Horae Synopticae,* Oxford, 1909), the authors of *Oxford Studies in the Synoptic Problem* (ed., W. Sanday, Oxford, 1911) and B. H. Streeter (*The Four Gospels,* London, 1924) can be blithely dismissed in a few pages.

[11] *RGG,* third ed., s.v. "Evangelien."

THE Q MATERIAL

Some of the views of the post-Bultmann school are a little surprising. The Q material represents the oldest written stratum in the gospels, earlier, that is, than Mark. In fact they come pretty close to the view of Taylor and T. W. Manson, that it should be dated about A.D. 50. Perhaps the sayings of Jesus were already being collected in Aramaic even prior to this date.[12] In support of an early date for the Q material the following considerations are offered: The Jewish people with their organized life around the Temple in Palestine are still a going concern. John the Baptist and the Pharisees still pose vital problems for the Christian community. The Q form of the missionary charge still confines the apostolic mission to Israel and does not yet envisage its extension to the Gentiles. This of course is not to say that the Gentile mission was wholly contrary to the outlook of Jesus or of the earliest Palestinian church (on this question see the preceding chapter, pp. 63f.). The common view that Q contains only *didache,* ethical teaching and not kerygma, is called in question. Q also contains preaching and shows that alongside of the post-Easter proclamation of Jesus as the redemptive act of God the earliest church also continued Jesus' own preaching of the kingdom of God. Of course this does not mean that the death and resurrection were

[12] In an interesting and significant article in the collected volume of essays entitled *Der historische Jesus und der kerygmatische Christus,* ed., H. Ristow and K. Matthiae, Berlin, 1961, pp. 342–370, H. Schürmann has put forward strong arguments for believing that some (not all) of the Q logia were collected during the life-time of Jesus and used by the disciples on their missions (Mark 6:7–13 par., Luke 10:1–12). If Schürmann is right these logia would have a pre-resurrection *Sitz im Leben,* a fact which would have very important consequences for the recovery of the *ipsissima verba* of Jesus. Unfortunately this book appeared too late for consideration in Chapter II.

simply ignored. As Tödt (see below, n. 13) argues, the very fact that the proclamation of Jesus was continued even after his death is an indication that the church which continued it believed that his preaching had been vindicated by God in the resurrection despite the Jews' rejection of it which culminated in the cross. So although there is no passion narrative and no mention of the resurrection in the Q material, its very existence presupposes both the passion and the resurrection. But at this stage (marked by the Q material on the one hand, and the earliest Christ-kerygma on the other, as evidenced in the speeches in the early chapters of Acts) no redemptive, atoning significance was as yet attached to the death of Jesus. Isa. 53 was not yet used to interpret the passion, but rather the Stone saying from Ps. 118:22f. (quoted in Mark 12:10f. and Acts 4:11). The passion was presented as the Jews' No to the eschatological proclamation of Jesus, the resurrection as God's Yes to that proclamation. This is the view of the passion and resurrection which, though not explicitly formulated in the Q material as it is in Mark and in the kerygmatic speeches of Acts, is nevertheless presupposed by it. The Q material expresses this vindication by God in the resurrection by identifying Jesus with the Son of man already in his earthly ministry, so that sayings are created (or perhaps modified from "I" sayings) in which Jesus speaks of himself already in his earthly ministry as Son of man. Thus the Q material already contains such sayings as:

> Foxes have holes, and the birds of the heaven have nests; but the Son of man has nowhere to lay his head.
>
> Matt. 8:20 par.

> The Son of man came eating and drinking.
>
> Matt. 11:19 par.

Whoever says a word against the Son of man shall be forgiven;
but whoever speaks against the Holy Spirit will not be forgiven.

Matt. 12:32 [13]

The kerygma of the earthly Jesus is now continued with the vindicated authority supplied by the resurrection. Hence Jesus already in his earthly ministry is called Son of man. But just as Q as yet contains no reflection about the redemptive significance of the passion, so too there is no reflection about the present status of Jesus after his exaltation and before his return. Yet adherence to Jesus' person remains, as it was already during his lifetime, decisive for one's acceptance or rejection by him when he returns. Thus the saying, Luke 12:8f. (which, as we have seen, the right wing post-Bultmannians still accept as authentically Jesuanic), is retained in the Q material, although these "future" Son of man sayings with their distinction between Jesus and the Son of man stand in tension with the "present" sayings. It is assumed, of course, that he who proclaimed his eschatological message on earth, and who will come again to vindicate the continuance of that message in the church is yet alive: but the connection between past and future, between the earthly Son of man and the transcendent Son of man who is to return has not yet been thought out.

[13] According to Tödt, *The Son of Man in the Synoptic Tradition*, pp. 118f., the meaning of this curious saying is that the Jews may have rejected Jesus (the Son of man) in his earthly ministry, and are now being given a second chance (in the church's kerygma). If they reject the church's kerygma (= the Holy Spirit) this rejection will be final. The saying clearly presupposes two periods—that of Jesus' earthly ministry and that of the church's kerygma.

MARK

Mark's gospel is the first *euangelion* proper, the first proclamation of Jesus as the Christ, crucified and risen. This proclamation of the church is combined with a reproduction of Jesus' own proclamation. In this combination Mark uses the narratives of Jesus' deeds in order to proclaim Jesus crucified and risen. These pericopes had of course been used in the oral tradition for kerygmatic purposes, that is to say, they had been used as vehicles to proclaim the Christ event as the redemptive act of God. Now, however, they are linked to the passion story and point forward to it. Each pericope becomes a prefiguration of what God does in the cross of Christ. So much for Mark's overall plan. A study of his redaction (the connecting links between the pericopes and their arrangement) leads to further detailed conclusions. For a sample of the results of this further study we turn now to the book by W. Marxsen (see above, p. 72, n. 2).

For Marxsen, Mark is writing in a very concrete situation, during the years 66–70 (once again we are surprised by this comparatively early dating). The Jerusalem church has fled to Galilee and is awaiting the parousia. All of Mark's references to Galilee throughout the gospel occur in the editorial sections, and therefore are of special importance to the evangelist. The time between the resurrection and parousia is a pause, not one of continuing significant history. It is the period of the Messianic woes which precede the end. Marxsen believes that the original tradition of the resurrection appearances located them at Jerusalem, and that Mark with his Galilean interests has deliberately changed them. But of course there are no resurrection appearances in Mark. This is deliberate. For what the disciples are told to go to

Galilee to see (Mark 16:7) is not the resurrection appearances, but the parousia. The command to "go" to Galilee reflects the flight of the Jerusalem church (in A.D. 66). Marxsen's emphasis on the Galilean tradition is not of course new. It was propounded in a series of works by Ernst Lohmeyer [14] and was taken up by R. H. Lightfoot.[15] There are some valuable insights in Marxsen's work, but the least convincing part is the theory that Mark's gospel is the product of Palestinian Christianity. That it has Palestinian tradition behind it is beyond doubt, but the language and thought (e.g., the Son of God Christology) are clear indications of its Hellenistic provenance.

We turn now to James M. Robinson's *The Problem of History in Mark* (see above, p. 72, n. 3). His thesis is that Mark's understanding of history is controlled by his eschatological outlook. It involves a succession of periods in redemptive history. (The work was written under O. Cullmann, before Dr. Robinson identified himself definitely with the post-Bultmannian school.) John the Baptist culminates the period of preparation begun in the Old Testament. The earthly ministry of Jesus is the final struggle between Satan and the Spirit-endowed Son of God. The temptation is the first round of that struggle. Then follow a series of conflicts—exorcisms, healings and debates with the Pharisees, altercations with the crowd and the battle with the blindness and obtuseness of the disciples. The conflict reaches its climax on the cross, where, however, the explicit motif of conflict is suppressed in the interests of

---

[14] *Galiläa und Jerusalem*, Göttingen, 1936; *Gottesknecht und Davidsohn*, Göttingen, 1945; and his two commentaries on Matthew (1958) and Mark (1954) in the Meyer series. ʻ

[15] *Locality and Doctrine in the Gospels*, London and New York, 1938; *The Gospel Message of St. Mark*, Oxford, 1951.

paradox. The little apocalypse serves as an open-ended pointer to the third period in redemptive history, the interval between the Christ event and the parousia. It is marked by the church's mission and the Messianic woes. The influence of Cullmann is unmistakable.

THE MESSIANIC SECRET

There has also been some interesting discussion on the Messianic secret in Mark. William Wrede, who first coined the term,[16] held that it was a device invented by Mark in order to reconcile the non-Messianic material of his sources with his own Christological beliefs. Jesus never regarded himself as Messiah or was during his earthly lifetime ever accepted as such: the Messianic faith began with the resurrection. Wrede's theory is reproduced almost exactly by Bultmann fifty years later in his *Theology of the New Testament* I, p. 32. Meanwhile, presence of the Messianic secret in Mark had come to be widely recognized by British scholars,[17] but they rejected Wrede's explanation of it. The Messianic secret was for them a historical fact. Jesus played down his miracles because he did not want to become known as a wonderworker, and forbad the demons and the disciples to make known his Messiahship because it would convey false, political notions of Messiahship. For Jesus interpreted his Messiahship in terms of the suffering servant. He did not wish it therefore to be publicized until after the passion, when its meaning was clear and it was safe to do so. There are also certain Continental scholars who uphold

[16] *Das Messiasgeheimnis in den Evangelien,* Göttingen, 1901.
[17] See, e.g., Vincent Taylor, *The Gospel According to St. Mark,* London, 1952, pp. 122–124; C. E. B. Cranfield, *The Gospel According to Saint Mark,* Cambridge, 1959, pp. 78f.

the historicity of the Messianic secret, but give a somewhat different explanation of it.[18] These scholars link it with the concept of the hidden, pre-existent Son of man as portrayed in the Similitudes of Enoch and in the fourth book of Ezra. The concept of hiddenness is transferred as it were from pre-existence to earthly life, though in each case the Son of man is awaiting his manifestation at the parousia in Enoch and IV Ezra, and at the resurrection or parousia in the gospels.

These attempts to rescue the historicity of the Messianic secret are rejected by the post-Bultmannian scholars. The reason is that the secrecy motif is to be found not in the pre-Marcan pericopes, but in the Marcan redactions. The secrecy motif is therefore the creation of Mark himself. Thus far Wrede and Bultmann are right. If the Messianic secret were historical it would certainly have to be contained within the pre-Marcan pericopes. And so Taylor, etc., are wrong. But the explanation which Wrede and Bultmann gave for the Messianic secret is wrong too. It could not have sprung from a desire to reconcile non-Christological material with Christological faith, since the pre-Marcan pericopes had long ago been impregnated with Christology, and the originally non- (or pre-) Messianic character of Jesus' history had long since been forgotten. The Christology is in the tradition, not in the redaction. What then is the purpose of the secrecy motif?

It serves rather to present in positive terms a concept of revelation conceived in terms of paradox. It is significant

[18] E.g., the two books by Erik Sjöberg, *Der Menschensohn im äthiopischen Henochbuch*, Lund, 1946, and *Der verborgene Menschensohn in den Evangelien*, Lund, 1955. J. Schniewind in his commentaries on Mark in *NT Deutsch*, Lohmeyer in his commentary on Matthew (above, p. 79, n. 14) and also to some extent Dibelius, use the same explanation of the secret, but are less confident of its historicity.

that Mark, who is certainly the creator of the theory, was most concerned to emphasize the motif of secrecy just where, in the pre-Marcan stage, the material had been impregnated most strongly with Christology, e.g., in the Transfiguration narrative (Mark 9:9).[19]

We might almost say that the secrecy motif, far from being designed to heighten the Christology, actually tones it down. It is perhaps the inevitable consequence of combining the pericopes with the passion-resurrection narrative. On their own, and as used in the preaching, the pericopes were sufficient proclamations in the church of the risen Christ. When tied down to the historical life of Jesus they would otherwise appear as direct revelations of the redemptive act of God during his earthly life. Hence the constant reminder that the earthly deeds of Christ are only prefigurations of revelation of the exalted Christ. In the last resort—and here the British scholars are ultimately right—the Messianic secret *is* historical, though not in the sense in which they mean it. It is historical in the sense that this is precisely the meaning of the history of Jesus, seen in the light of the resurrection.

MATTHEW

The new concern for the evangelists as creative writers seems to have begun with Matthew, and outside the post-Bultmannian school, in the books by G. D. Kilpatrick [20] and Krister Stendahl.[21] Kilpatrick stresses the liturgical origin and purpose of St. Matthew's Gospel, while Stendahl's thesis is that it is the product of a Christian school (he has not yet

[19] H. Conzelmann, art., "Jesus Christus," in *RGG*, third ed.
[20] *The Origins of the Gospel According to St. Matthew*, Oxford, 1946.
[21] *The School of St. Matthew*, Uppsala, 1954.

broken away from the "socialist" view of the gospels), like the schools of the Rabbis, or perhaps even like the scriptorium at Qumran. In fact, the parallel with Qumran is even closer, and affects the theology of St. Matthew. For he presents Jesus as the true expositor of the Torah, whose work was thus formally analogous to that of the Teacher of Righteousness, the founder of the Qumran community. Matthew betrays his method in Matt. 13:52: "Every scribe enrolled as a disciple in the kingdom of God is like a man, a householder, who produces from his treasury new things and old things."

The strictly post-Bultmannian study of Matthew opened with Günther Bornkamm's essay in the Dodd *Festschrift* (see above, p. 2, note 3). This essay is devoted to three main themes. First, Matthew's Christology. Jesus is presented in his earthly life as the one who is the humiliated king, fulfilling the Old Testament prophecies concerning Emmanuel, Bethlehem, Galilee and the Servant (Matt. 1:22f., 2:5f., 4:14f., 12:17ff.). His mission on earth is to Israel, but since Israel rejects him there is launched after the resurrection a world-wide mission of *teaching*. Secondly, Matthew's doctrine of the church. As is well known, the term *ecclesia,* church, occurs only in Matthew among the four gospels (Matt. 16:18, 18:17). Jesus is the second Moses, who brings the authentic exposition of the Mosaic law—not actually a new law as such (cf. Stendahl above)—to his *ecclesia,* a community organized under the new righteousness which exceeds the righteousness of the scribes and Pharisees. This leads us to the third aspect of Matthew's theology—his eschatology. Mark had been expecting an imminent parousia (cf. Marxsen above). Matthew, however, is beginning to envisage a further period of history, marked by the church's mission, a period which is more than just a pause before the end filled out by the Messianic woes, as in Mark 13. This interval, it is true, is not filled with such positive content as it is in Luke (see below). It is hardly yet a distinct phase in salvation existing in its own right, and with its own distinctive features. Nevertheless, the evident delay in the parousia receives special emphasis in Matthew and makes the organized life of the Christian ecclesia the preparation for the end. It is significant that the last judgment, with which Matthew is so much preoccupied, is directed not against the Jews who reject Jesus' eschatological proclamation, but is to be passed on the church according as its members have lived obedient to the law of the righteousness of the kingdom of heaven. The great discourses which are so striking a feature of St. Matthew's gospel, the sermon on the mount (chapters 5–7), the missionary charge (chapter 10), the parable discourse (chapter 13), the community discourse (chapter 18) and the eschatological discourse (chapters 24–25) lay down conditions for entry into the eschatological kingdom of God. The church lives under the shadow of the last judgment, and its life must be ordered accordingly in the light of Jesus' teaching on the new righteousness.

Here we have the beginning of the process which is taken further in Luke, and which reaches its culmination in the early catholicism of the second century. The church is no longer an interim community waiting to take off at any moment. It is here to stay, at any rate for the time being, and must settle down to organize its life in the world. Matthew is feeling his way towards a conception of Jesus as the inaugurator of a new phase in redemptive history. There had been the period of promise (the Old Testament), the period of fulfilment in humiliation (the earthly ministry of Jesus), and now there is the period of the mission and of the organized life of the ecclesia under the Torah as expounded by Jesus. Then will come the End, when the church will be judged by the authentic interpretation of the Torah. This comes out with especial clarity in the interpretation to the parable on the wheat and tares (Matt. 13:36–43), which J. Jeremias has convincingly shown [22] is a Matthean construct, and the scene of the last judgment in Matt. 25:31–46, which if not Matthew's own composition has at least been heavily worked over by him. Although the post-Bultmannian scholars do not go as far as the Swiss liberals,[23] who find the whole clue to the development of Christian dogma in the delay of the parousia, they do at least regard it as *one* important clue in the process which led to the "earthly catholicism" of the second century.

[22] *The Parables of Jesus,* London and New York, 1963, pp. 81–85.
[23] E.g., M. Werner, *The Formation of Christian Dogma,* London, 1957.

VI

The Lucan Writings

TWO IMPORTANT STUDIES on Luke and Acts have emerged from the Bultmann school. Hans Conzelmann's *Theology of St. Luke* (see above, p. 72, n. 4) and Ernst Haenchen's commentary on Acts in the tenth edition of the Meyer series.[1]

CONZELMANN ON ST. LUKE

While Conzelmann's work does not deal directly with source analysis, his exposition rests very heavily on cer-

[1] *Die Apostelgeschichte*, Kritisch-exegetischer Kommentar, Göttingen, 1954. It has already been issued in a revised edition in 1959.

tain conclusions in this field. He rejects the proto-Luke theory in any form. This enables him to attribute a greater creative contribution to the evangelist himself. For example, the position of the rejection at Nazareth is not due to a proto-Luke, but is Luke's own deliberate alteration of his Marcan source; and the expansion of this Marcan pericope is due, not to an alternative source, but to Luke's own editing of Mark. This is typical of Conzelmann's treatment of Luke throughout. His attribution of so much to the creative activity of the evangelist seems on the one hand to result in a skeptical view of the gospel as a source for the history of Jesus, but it does serve on the other hand to make Luke stand out as one of the creative theologians of the New Testament. It is a reaction against older views which regarded him either as a scissors and paste redactor (source criticism) or as a mere collector of oral tradition (form criticism). Luke's modification of Mark discloses to us his fundamental theological concept. This is a threefold periodization of redemptive history. Period I is the time of Israel, the time of the law and the prophets. Period II is the life of Jesus, in fulfilment of period I. Period III is the period of the church, between the ascension of Jesus and his *parousia*. St. Luke's gospel deals with the middle period, and hence the title of the German original of Conzelmann's book, which means "The Middle of Time." The English title has lost this succinct allusion to Conzelmann's thesis. This middle period in turn is itself divided into three phases. The first is marked by the call of Jesus and the summoning of the witnesses (3:1–9:50). The second expounds the necessity of the passion (9:51–19:27). The third comprises the journey to Jerusalem and the passion (19:28–end). The reader will notice with some surprise that the so-called "travel document," "Samaritan section" or "Perean section" has gone.

Conzelmann maintains that Jesus does not leave Galilee until Luke 19:28, and that the idea of a travel section has been unwarrantably read into Luke. Within the three periods themselves Conzelmann carefully analyzes the redactional framework and finds that Luke's geography is not meant to be historically informative (Luke has as a matter of fact only the vaguest notions about the geography of Palestine) but symbolic and theological. Certain geographical locations are associated with certain types of teaching or incident. Thus the mountain is the place of communication between Jesus and the heavenly world. It is a place to which the crowds have no access (e.g., the mountain in the Transfiguration story). The sea, similarly, is the place for epiphanies of Jesus' power to the disciples—and again the crowds have no access to the sea. The desert is the place of conflict with Satan. Finally, the level plain is the place of Jesus' contact with the crowds. The location of the traditions serves to indicate their significance to the evangelist. Specific geography, e.g., Galilee, Samaria, Jerusalem, also has theological significance. Perhaps this is the most far-fetched and least convincing part of Conzelmann's otherwise penetrating and suggestive study. In fact, he has been accused of making Luke a gnostic![2]

Another notable feature of Conzelmann's treatment is, as we have seen, that he denies the existence of the so-called travel or Samaritan section. There is no real travel in Luke 9:51–19:27. The appearance is altogether illusory, and is due to Luke's geographical symbolism. Indeed, contrary to the usual assumption, the Lucan Jesus never actually sets foot in Samaria—and this for theological reasons! On the subject of Luke's treatment of the Messianic secret in his Marcan source, Conzelmann makes the interesting point that

[2] See the review by P. Winter in *ThLZ*, 81, 1956, Nr. 1, p. 38.

whereas in Mark the secret consists in the *fact* of the Messiah-ship, in Luke it is the *mode* of the Messiahship. This is what is disclosed to the disciples after Caesarea Philippi. The pathway to Messianic glory lies through Messianic suffering.

The undoubted crudities and at times even absurdities in this pioneer work should not blind us to its real significance. Luke has often been given less credit than he deserves as an evangelist—he has been called the dim wit among the evangelists.[3] Luke has been regarded mainly as a historian—a sound one by conservatives and a fallible one by radicals—but still a historian and not an evangelist. Now, however, he is beginning to emerge as a theologian in his own right. Secondly, Luke is emerging as a theologian of the sub-apostolic age. Like Matthew, he stands at the threshold of the development which in the second century crystallized into early catholicism, but is already a little further across that threshold than Matthew. The parousia hope is fading, the church has come to stay and must settle down in this world as a factor in civilization. Note for instance the omission of Mark 1:15 which speaks of the imminence of the Kingdom of God. Note also the elaborate dating of Luke 3:1f. The Christ event is set in the context of secular and world history. Note finally the treatment of Mark's Little Apocalypse (Mark 13) in Luke 21, especially verse 20: in Luke the Messianic woes of Mark have become historical events which have already occurred. Luke 21:20 is not simply to be labelled as a *vaticinium ex eventu* referring to the siege of Jerusalem in A.D. 70, nor simply used as evidence for the date of Luke. It is an important clue to his whole out-

[3] I owe this phrase to Prof. G. W. H. Lampe, now of Cambridge. On the alleged "early catholicism" of the Lucan writings, see also C. K. Barrett, *Luke the Historian in Recent Study*, London, 1961. Barrett does not take too kindly to this view—particularly, I think, because he shrinks from the notion that "catholicism" should have a foothold in the canon. See also below, p. 95.

look. True, the parousia still lies ahead. There is still to be a consummation. But the parousia is not imminent. It does not decisively determine and control the present, as it did for Jesus and the earliest church. It merely rounds off the third phase of redemptive history. It is already being relegated to its place as the last chapter in Christian dogmatics. Christianity is rather seen as the working out of God's purpose in a redemptive history. And alongside of this new emphasis on history, Jesus' activity is seen not so much as *euangelion,* eschatological message. Luke uses the verb *euangelizesthai* for Jesus' own proclamation, but never the noun, either for Jesus' own message or for his life regarded as the eschatological act of God. It is significant that he calls his work not *euangelion,* as Mark does (Mark 1:1), but *diegesis,* narrative. Although it is now almost commonplace that the gospels are proclamations of Jesus, not biographies, Luke's gospel does come closer than any of the others to being a life of Jesus.

Much of Conzelmann's thesis rests on the generally accepted assumption that the gospel is continued by a second work by the same writer, the Book of Acts. This assumption has been variously questioned in certain quarters. For instance P. Winter, in the review of Conzelmann mentioned above (p. 88, n. 2), has resuscitated Burkitt's view that Acts was meant to be followed by a third volume. On the other hand my colleague, Dr. Jules L. Moreau, maintains that the gospel was published alone. When Acts was later published by a different author it was prefaced by what is now the introduction to Luke. Then, when the two works were combined, Dr. Moreau thinks, the original preface of Acts was transferred to become the preface to the gospel and a new preface constructed for the second volume. On either of these views the basic assumption on which Conzelmann erects his thesis, that Luke presents Jesus as the middle of time, falls to the ground. But I think that neither of these views need be taken seriously. Luke's gospel quite unequivocally points forward to Acts, and Acts points forward just as clearly to no other event save the parousia itself.

HAENCHEN ON LUKE

In his commentary on Acts Ernst Haenchen generally accepts Conzelmann's periodization of the Lucan theology. For him Luke, unlike Mark and Matthew, is a consciously literary work, though even Matthew does of course improve Mark's Greek. Like the secular historians of the age Luke starts his work with a conventional prologue. For Haenchen too, Luke's gospel is the first life of Jesus. It represents Christianity's first contact with the world of culture, as is indicated by the interest of Acts in the Greco-Roman world, and particularly by St. Paul's speech at the Areopagus. For Haenchen too, Luke has abandoned the imminent hope of the parousia. The Neronian persecution already lies some years back, and can therefore no longer be identified with the woes which usher in the end. The place of John the Baptist in the Christian scheme has changed. He is no longer identified with Elijah, a point which is also emphasized by A. R. C. Leaney in his commentary on Luke,[4] though without any clear indication of the theological reason for this change. The reason is that it is necessary to play down John in view of the advanced claims now being made for him by his followers. This trend is carried still further in the fourth gospel.

[4] *A Commentary on the Gospel According to St. Luke,* London and New York, 1958.

DIBELIUS: THE TURNING POINT

We turn now to Acts itself. The year 1923 may be said to mark a turning point in the study of Acts. It had been the achievement of the liberal scholars, notably of Harnack and Johannes Weiss, to have finally overthrown the *Tendenz-kritik* of F. C. Baur and the Tübingen school. But the study of Acts in the age of Harnack had been preoccupied with the question of literary sources and with the corresponding treatment of Acts itself as source material for the beginnings of Christianity. Estimates of the value of this source material varied. For the conservative scholars it was very valuable information, for the radicals much less so, but both agreed that the primary importance of Acts was what it told us about the history of the earliest church. In 1923, however, Martin Dibelius published the first of a series of essays which have recently been collected in a posthumous volume entitled *Aufsätze zur Apostelgeschichte*.[5] These essays are an attempt to apply the form critical method to Acts. Dibelius observes that unlike the gospels Acts contains no paradigms. The reason for this is that the church did not preach the apostles as they preached Jesus. It is therefore quite wrong to suppose that Luke used the same methods of composition in Acts as he did for the gospel, an erroneous assumption which dominated the study of Acts in the age of Harnack. Hence we should not look in Acts either for orally transmitted pericopes or for written sources of the type Luke used in the gospel. Acts was Luke's own composition. He was a pioneer in the field and had to create his own literary

[5] Göttingen, 1951. E. tr., *Studies in the Acts of the Apostles* by Mary Ling, London, New York, 1956.

form. Indeed, conditions prior to the writing of Acts were hardly suitable to encourage such an enterprise. A church which was looking forward to a speedy End was not likely to be particularly interested in its past. Mark, for instance, as we have seen, conceives the history of the post-Easter church, marked by persecution and witness, as only a brief interval before the End. It was only as the hope of an imminent parousia failed and as the church consequently settled down in this world (the sense of which is, as we have already seen, a dominant feature of Luke's gospel), that it occurred, or could have occurred, to anyone to write a history of the church. This is not, however, to say that Luke had no sources, but only to deny that the sources he used had already been used for the purpose to which he puts them, viz., for a connected history of the early church. He did in fact have one continuous source, namely the famous travel diary which underlies the latter part of Acts. He had also other pre-existing material of various kinds, "legends," i.e., stories about individuals such as Tabitha, Cornelius, the Ethiopian eunuch, Ananias and Sapphira, etc. There were also what Dibelius calls "profane stories" such as the account of Herod Agrippa's death in chapter 12, the Eutychus episode in chapter 20, the story of the sons of Sceva, and the escape of Paul and Silas from the jail at Philippi. There was also, Dibelius thinks, an itinerary covering travels outside the travel diary proper, and including the middle chapters of Acts. Even when all this material has been accounted for by the use of sources, it still leaves a great deal to the creative work of the author of Acts himself. He is responsible for the generalizing summaries which punctuate the narrative, for the working up of the "legends," for the connecting links between one episode and another, and most important of all, for the speeches. These, Dibelius maintains, are examples of Christian preaching, both kerygmatic (evangelistic) and apologetic, such as was in use at the time when Acts itself was written (c. A.D. 90). Yet, despite this attribution of so much to the creativity of the author, and the consequent result that Acts is more useful as evidence for the church of A.D. 90 than for the Apostolic age, Dibelius still maintained the traditional authorship of the work. It was still the product of a companion of St. Paul. How then could a companion of St. Paul have created his material so freely, not from his memories of the past, but from his experiences of the present? The answer, according to Dibelius, is that at the time when he accompanied Paul he had no intention of writing an Acts. After all, he probably thought that he, like Paul, would shortly see the parousia! Also, the author of Acts is not writing merely as a reporter. An ancient historian was not a kind of photographer, but more like a portrait painter. He dealt with the typical rather than with the concrete.

Dibelius' essays marked a new phase in the study of Acts, so that in this field of study we may rightly speak of the post-Dibelian period. What are the generally agreed results of his work? First, there is general agreement to abandon the quest for written sources in Acts. Gone are the days of "Jerusalem source A," "Jerusalem source B" and the "Antiochene source" of the Harnackian era, at least as written documents. Secondly, it is clear that in speaking of Luke as a historian we cannot mean it in the nineteenth century sense of the word. All that remains of Harnack's position in the hands of Dibelius is the traditional view of the Lucan authorship—and even that remains as a kind of useless appendix, not exploited in any decisive way for the historical evaluation of Acts as a whole.

THE POST-DIBELIAN ERA

Advancing from Dibelius' positions, the post-Dibelians are paying close attention to the theology of Acts: not to the theology of the apostolic age which it allegedly presents, but to the theology of the author himself. That is to say, they are concerning themselves with precisely those elements which Dibelius had attributed to the creativity of the author—the speeches, generalizing summaries and connecting links, and the shaping up of the earlier material.

The first effort in this direction was an article by Philipp Vielhauer "On the Paulinism of Acts." [6] By comparing Luke's outlook with Paul's, this writer shows that the author of Acts belongs definitely to the post- (or sub-) apostolic age. Unlike Paul, for instance, Luke sets great store by natural theology. He does not understand the profound psychological and theological reasons which underlay Paul's opposition to the law as a way to salvation. Luke plays down the cross: it has not that decisive significance as the saving event *par excellence* that it has for Paul. Finally, Luke has abandoned the expectation of an imminent parousia.

While E. Käsemann has apparently written no monograph devoted exclusively to Acts, he makes a number of incidental remarks on that book in published work on other subjects in some of his articles in *Zeitschrift für Theologie und Kirche*. Acts, for Käsemann as for other members of this school, represents the beginnings of "early catholicism," a development which had generally been assigned exclusively to the second century, and outside the canonical scriptures. "Early catholicism" thus has a definite foothold within the canon—an important point which incidentally has far-reaching implications for contemporary ecumenical discussion.

[6] German, 1950. E. tr. in *The Perkins School of Theology Journal*, 17 (1963), pp. 5–17.

HAENCHEN ON ACTS

We have already had occasion to note the important commentary on Acts by E. Haenchen (see above, p. 91). We now turn to what he has to say about Acts:

> Hitherto Acts has been read and studied chiefly for information about the Apostolic age. The only question was, how far that information was reliable. Now we are beginning to see that it is a work of art, not a straightforward narrative, and that properly to appreciate it we must understand the principles of its composition.
>
> At the same time we are coming to realize that Acts contains a theology which, whether we like it or not, must be taken seriously. This is what will determine the study of Acts in the years that lie ahead.[7]

What is this theology of Acts as Haenchen sees it? In answering this question he follows closely the suggestions of Conzelmann's earlier work on Luke (see above, p. 72 n. 4). Acts covers a third epoch in redemptive history. The middle period, that of Jesus, has been succeeded by the period of the church. There are, moreover, two phases in the period after Jesus, the time of the apostles and a time after the apostles, the period in which Luke himself stands. The apostolic age he regards as the norm and ideal. It was a time when there was no false doctrine, as there was in the subsequent age. Here Paul's speech to the elders at Ephesus in chapter 20 provides important evidence for Luke's perspective. But the apostolic age was not just to be contemplated and admired. It is the ground of the church's existence in Luke's own time. Therefore one of his primary motives in writing Acts was *edification*—for the church of his own day.

As for the sources of Acts, it is to be noted that there was

[7] Haenchen, *op. cit.*, p. 41.

no tradition of the sayings of the apostles, as there was for the sayings of Jesus—only a few *praxeis,* doings of Peter and Paul, and to a lesser degree of such minor figures as Philip the Evangelist. Luke also had an "itinerary"—not identical with the we-sections of the travel diary, to which Haenchen adopts a somewhat equivocal attitude. The itinerary is difficult to reconstruct because of Luke's own additions to it.

Next, Haenchen turns to Luke's own contributions. The chief of these (cf. Dibelius) is the speeches, eight of which are put into the mouth of Peter, and nine into the mouth of Paul. With a number even of British scholars,[8] and like Dibelius himself, Haenchen thinks that the speeches in Acts are Lucan compositions. Haenchen notes that a constantly recurring pattern is discernible in the kerygmatic speeches. First they set forth the Christ event. Second, there is a scriptural proof to demonstrate that in the Christ event God is fulfilling the promises of the Old Covenant. Third, it is claimed that the apostles are witnesses of these things. Fourth, and finally, there is a challenge to repent and believe. There is no guarantee that this pattern goes back to the apostolic age. Rather, it reflects the missionary preaching current around the year A.D. 90. The semitisms of these speeches, which had long been the chief argument in favor of their antiquity,[9] are due rather to the conscious use of the Septuagint,[10] or in some instances are echoes of liturgical formulae. With this last concession we may compare Eduard Schweizer's valuable article on the speeches in Acts.[11] Schweizer recognizes the use of older material in the specifi-

---

[8] E.g., C. F. Evans' article in *JTS* cited above, p. 2, n. 2.

[9] C. H. Dodd, following de Zwaan's modification of C. C. Torrey, held that some of these speeches are translations from the Aramaic: *The Apostolic Preaching and Its Developments* (see above, p. 2, n. 2), pp. 19f., esp. 20, n. 1.

[10] Cf. H. F. D. Sparks, "The Semitisms of Acts," in *JTS* n.s. 1, 1950, pp. 16–28.

[11] "Zu den Reden der Apostelgeschichte," *ThZ,* 13, 1957, pp. 1–11.

cally *Christological* parts of the kerygmatic speeches. This is a highly important modification of the thesis that the speeches are Lucan compositions, and indeed gives us what we really want from these speeches, namely evidence for the Christology of the earliest church.

Turning with Haenchen to the non-kerygmatic speeches, we have first of all Paul's farewell discourses to the elders at Ephesus (Acts 20:18–35). Here Paul is presented as the ideal missionary and church leader. The whole speech reflects the concern of the sub-apostolic church with the growth of false teaching (cf. the "fierce wolves" of v. 29). Then there are a number of apologetic speeches directed against Judaism on the one hand and at the Roman government on the other. These endeavor to present Christianity as the true Judaism and thus to claim for it the status of a *religio licita* such as orthodox Judaism also enjoyed in the eyes of the imperial authorities. Such recognition would secure the church from liability to sporadic outbursts of persecution such as were becoming increasingly common toward the end of the first century.[12]

The second contribution of the author of Acts is his expansion of the itineraries. For example, the story of Paul at Athens is based on an earlier itinerary, which certainly contained 17:17a. But the Areopagus speech is a purely Lucan construction, contradicting as it does the procedure of the historical Paul as recounted in I Cor. 2:3–5:

> And I was with you in much weakness and in much fear and trembling; and my speech and my message were not in plausible words of wisdom, but in demonstration of

[12] On this alleged apologetic motif in Acts, cf. also B. S. Easton, "The Purpose of Acts," in *Early Christianity*, ed., F. C. Grant, Greenwich, 1954, pp. 33–118. Haenchen's espousal of Easton's thesis has not won general acceptance among his fellow post-Dibelians.

the Spirit and power, that your faith might not rest in the wisdom of men but in the power of God.

The Lucan speech, however, portrays a self-conscious encounter between the kerygma and the culture of the Greek world—the beginnings of the kind of thing we find in the second century apologists.

The third element contributed by the author himself, namely the generalizing summaries, are designed to mark the progress of the gospel in the Roman world. They show "how we got where we are today"—from the obscure origins of the Jewish sect in Palestine.

On the question of authorship, Haenchen first points out that Luke does not regard Paul as an apostle on the same level as the Twelve. The historical Paul on the other hand claimed to be an apostle in the fullest sense, of equal authority with the Twelve, a claim which was apparently recognized by the Twelve themselves (I Cor. 9:1, 15:9; Gal. 1-2). This change of perspective is characteristic of the sub-apostolic age, in which the term "apostle" is being increasingly restricted to the Twelve.[13] The antithesis between Pauline and Jewish Christianity is completely redefined. There are, it is true, traces of the controversy over the law, which had occupied so much of Paul's attention in Romans and Galatians; but Paul's opponents here are mainly Jews, not Judaizing Christians. Paul's opposition to Judaism, similarly, has shifted its ground. It is not against the law as a way of salvation, for the sub-apostolic age was becoming increasingly moralistic as we may see from I Clement, Didache, etc., but merely

---

[13] Two recent studies (G. Klein, *Die Zwölf Apostel,* and W. Schmithals, *Das kirchliche Apostelamt,* both Göttingen, 1961) argue that originally the Twelve were *not* apostles. Klein thinks that Acts first called them so, and that this is part of its "early catholicism."

against Sadduccism, on such comparatively trivial doctrinal points as the Spirit, angels and the resurrection. This redefinition of the Pauline conflict fits in with the apologetic motif. Christianity is displayed as a legitimate form of Judaism, and therefore entitled to the status of a *religio licita*. Now in the light of all this it is difficult, Haenchen concludes, to believe, as even Dibelius still believed, that Luke was a companion of Paul, or even his contemporary. The work bears all the marks of the post-Pauline period, and betrays the hand of one who only knew Paul himself from a distance.

What, finally, about the provenance and date of Acts? Here Haenchen has no startling suggestion to make. He is inclined to think that the work reflects the political conditions in the last decade of the first century (cf. the remarks about persecution in the reign of Domitian, above, p. 98). He is also inclined to view with favor B. H. Streeter's speculation that Theophilus, to whom Luke-Acts is dedicated, was intended as a pseudonym for Flavius Clemens.[14] Acts may have emanated from Greece, a fact suggested by the prominence accorded to Athens and to Athenian culture in chapter 17. Perhaps this is the truth behind the legend that "Luke" died at Thebes.

[14] See B. H. Streeter, *The Four Gospels,* London, 1924, pp. 535ff.

VII

The Johannine Problem

IN ORDER TO PUT the contemporary discussion of the Johannine problem in its proper perspective let us first recall the course of the debate during the present century. In 1900 the liberals and the conservatives were in deadlock. The conservatives were confident that the fourth gospel was the work of John bar Zebedee, a historical account by an eyewitness of the ministry of Jesus. The classic formulation of this thesis was Westcott's "concentric proof." [1] The author of the fourth gospel was a Jew, a Jew of Palestine, an eyewitness, and apostle, the apostle John. On the other hand the liberals were equally confident that the fourth gospel was the product of

[1] B. F. Westcott, *The Gospel According to St. John,* London, 1908, pp. x–lii.

Hellenistic mysticism, written perhaps about the middle of the second century. After the first world war something of a rapprochement took place. The conservatives had by now come to accept the critical solution of the synoptic problem, with the result that they were now dominated by literary hypotheses concerning gospel origins. It became apparent to them therefore that John's gospel stood in a literary relationship, certainly with Mark, probably with Luke, and possibly also with Matthew. Hence the fourth gospel, even for the conservatives, could no longer be regarded directly as the work of an eyewitness or an apostle. They fell back therefore on various views of mediate apostolic authorship, the commonest theory being that it was the work of that somewhat shadowy figure, John the Elder or Presbyter. The more conservative form of this view was that this John the Elder was directly dependent on the tradition of John the Apostle, which enabled him to supplement, and at times even to correct, the synoptic tradition.[2] A less conservative view was that of B. H. Streeter,[3] who maintained that the Elder used the traditions he had received (all three synoptists, plus a Jerusalem tradition) quite freely as the jumping off point for independent meditations on the meaning of Christ as he had come to perceive it in his own mystical experience. These independent contributions are to be seen particularly in the discourses, which are the free compositions of the evangelist. When for instance the Johannine Christ says, "I am the way, the truth, and the life," these are not the words of Jesus himself, but a Christian meditation on the meaning of the Lord, the equivalent of *"Thou* art the way, the truth, and the life." Thus in Bernard and Streeter respectively we see

[2] See J. H. Bernard, *The Gospel According to St. John,* pp. xlv–lix, cii–cvii, London, 1928, and New York, 1929.

[3] B. H. Streeter, *The Four Gospels,* London, 1924, pp. 430–461, 467–481.

the rapprochement between the conservative and liberal positions.

SURVIVALS OF CONSERVATISM

Of course, the older conservative view is still held in some quarters, even in its unmodified form. For instance, W. Temple in his highly valued *Readings in St. John's Gospel*[4] combined a very conservative view on the authorship and historical character of the gospel with a somewhat Platonizing exegesis. As an example of his conservatism we may instance his view that chapters 15–16 and even the high priestly prayer of chapter 17 were actually delivered not in the upper room but literally on the way to Gethsemane across the brook Cedron—this because of the words, "Rise, let us go hence," at the end of chapter 14 (!). Temple's reputation is so high that it is sometimes difficult to persuade even theological students and parochial clergy that his *Readings in St. John*, while of great devotional value, are not infallible in the realm of biblical scholarship. Archbishop Ramsey has observed that Temple was a philosopher who always remained something of an amateur as a theologian,[5] a judgment which applies with even greater force to his status as a biblical scholar. But the most extreme statement of the unreconstructed conservative position in recent years is that of R. A. Edwards, Canon of Norwich.[6] Edwards believes that the author was John the son of Zebedee, and puts up a vigorous defense of the external evidence: if the period between A.D. 100 and Irenaeus is shrouded in mist for us, there is no reason

---

[4] London, 1939–45.

[5] A. M. Ramsey, *An Era in Anglican Theology* (British title: *From Gore to Temple*), New York, London, 1960, p. 146.

[6] *The Gospel According to St. John*, London, 1954.

to suppose that it was for Irenaeus himself. He knew what he was talking about when he spoke of his links with St. John through Polycarp.[7] John, Edwards suggests (it is avowedly only an impression, not susceptible of proof), took notes of what Jesus said and did while the ministry was actually proceeding. Then, apparently the notes were stored away until, in old age, he was prevailed upon to write down (or dictate) his reminiscences, which he did in Greek,[8] as a defense of the gospel against docetism.[9] Thus the gospel is literal history. This view, however, is purchased at a price. Edwards throws overboard Clement of Alexandria's insight that this is a "spiritual gospel." [10] He rationalizes the miracle of the feeding of the five thousand by suggesting that the crowd shared their food they had brought with them, and that the "panic" of the disciples was unnecessary.[11] He plays down the theologizing element in the fourth gospel.[12] He will have no truck with symbolism, e.g., the symbolic interpretation of the catch of 153 fishes in John 21:11. All fishermen, especially when they are in partnership, count their catches! There is little future for this kind of conservatism. But, as we shall see later, the discovery of the Dead Sea Scrolls has opened up new possibilities that some of the conservative positions were right after all (see below, pp. 125ff.).

FOUR RECENT STUDIES

In 1940 there appeared E. C. Hoskyns' great commentary on St. John's Gospel.[13] Käsemann has described it as "the only really Barthian commentary on the fourth gospel,"

---

[7] *Ibid.*, pp. 3f.   [8] *Ibid.*, p. 15.   [9] *Ibid.*, pp. 16, 23.

[10] *Ibid.*, pp. 23, 192f.   [11] *Ibid.*, p. 57.

[12] Note his criticism of Westcott, *ibid.*, p. 44.

[13] *The Fourth Gospel*, London, 1940.

comparable to Barth's own commentary on the Epistle to the Romans in scope, style and import. Hoskyns had only completed his comments on the first six chapters of the gospel. The rest of the work was edited posthumously from Hoskyns' notes by his pupil F. N. Davey. For all its rugged eloquence, there is a certain serenity about this work which will make it timeless: critical views may change, but Hoskyns is so much above them, so sensitive to their ultimate unimportance, that his profound theological insight into the meaning of the gospel will never lose its relevance.

The next year, 1941, saw the appearance of another great commentary, that of R. Bultmann.[14] This work, we understand, is in process of translation into English. It raises all the main issues which are in the forefront of the Johannine discussion at the present time, and we shall deal with them all in turn.

In 1953, C. H. Dodd brought out his long-waited work, *The Interpretation of the Fourth Gospel*.[15] This is not an ordinary commentary, but an extended treatment of the Johannine problem, divided into three parts. The first part is a discussion of the affinities of the evangelist's thought. Dodd admits that the evangelist shows some acquaintance with Palestinian and Rabbinic Judaism, but contends that like Philo, though independently of him, his real sympathies lie with that "higher paganism" of the Hellenistic world evidenced by the (admittedly post-Johannine) Hermetic literature. The evangelist's purpose is missionary and apologetic: he seeks to commend the Christian kerygma to this world of higher Hellenistic paganism by restating it in acceptable terms. The second part of Dodd's work is a series

[14] *Das Johannesevangelium* (the 10th edition in the Meyer Commentary), Göttingen, 1941.

[15] Cambridge.

of word studies on the Wörterbuch method.[16] The key concepts of the fourth gospel, light, life, truth, etc., are analyzed in respect of their antecedents in the Hebrew Bible, the Septuagint, in Classical Greek and in Hellenism, and of their usage in the fourth gospel itself. The third part of the book is devoted to an analysis of the structure of the gospel itself, together with an exposition of its argument as a connected whole.

The fourth monumental work to be mentioned at this point is C. K. Barrett's commentary.[17] As the first full-scale commentary on the Greek text to be published in English since Bernard (1928) its appearance was an event of considerable importance. It opens, as most English commentaries do, with a full introduction, comprising six chapters: (1) The Gospel, its Characteristics and Purpose, (2) The Non-Christian Background of the Gospel; (3) The Christian Background of the Gospel; (4) The Theology of the Gospel; (5) The Origin and Authority of the Gospel; (6) The Text. Barrett was a pupil of Dodd at Cambridge, and although Dodd's work appeared two years after Barrett had finished his manuscript [18] it obviously bears the mark of Dodd's influence, especially of the lectures given by Dodd at Cambridge in 1937, which the present writer also attended. This influence is particularly apparent in the section on the non-Christian background of the gospel. Like Dodd, Barrett thinks that the evangelist's chief non-Christian affinities are with the higher paganism of the Hellenistic world. Like

---

[16] I.e., the method employed in the *Theologisches Wörterbuch zum Neue Testament,* vols. I and II of which are now in E. tr. (Grand Rapids, 1964).

[17] C. K. Barrett, *The Gospel According to St. John,* London, 1955.

[18] The MS. was finished in 1951: the book was not published until 1955. This has to be remembered in any assessment of Barrett's work.

Dodd in 1937, Barrett believes that John certainly knew Mark, probably knew Luke, and possibly knew Matthew. Barrett minimizes the Palestinian, Aramaic affinities of the gospel: the utmost he will concede is that the author, while writing in Greek, was bilingual. The Dead Sea Scrolls appeared too late for the author to consider them as part of the possible non-Christian background, but, writing in 1955 [19] he states that the Qumran discoveries would not have substantially modified his work. For all its value—and the commentary especially is marked by a high degree of scholarly judiciousness—Barrett's work, as we shall see, remains now a little old-fashioned, for the trend of scholarly opinion on the relation of John and the synoptists, on its non-Christian affinities and on its dating,[20] was already running against Barrett in 1951, and more so since 1955. Above all his view that the work is essentially a product of Hellenistic Christianity has been seriously, and with grounds, called into question during the last decade. All these points will be noted in the ensuing discussion.

CURRENT TRENDS:

I. AUTHORSHIP

We will now proceed to examine some of these current trends in Johannine studies. As compared with the earlier period (say, prior to 1940) there has been a marked loss of interest in the problem of the gospel's authorship. True, there are still a few who are concerned, as in the period between the wars, to uphold the theory that the gospel is the work of John the Elder, or in some other way to maintain a medi-

[19] Preface, p. viii, n. 1.
[20] Barrett puts the *terminus ad quem* at 140, which is undoubtedly too late. See below, p. 110.

ate apostolic authorship.[21] Insofar as it is raised at all, it plays only a peripheral part in the wider discussion of the authority of the gospel. Thus Hoskyns was content to acknowledge that the author was one "created by the apostolic witness and formed by apostolic obedience" to such a degree that "he was veritably carried across into the company of the original disciples and invested with the authority of their mission." [22] Or again, the question of authorship comes up in the discussion of the affinities of the evangelist's thought. It is in this context that Dodd contents himself with the conclusion that the author was an unknown Christian of the second generation at Ephesus.[23] Barrett devotes pp. 105-114 in his introduction to a discussion of "Date, Place and Authorship." His concluding paragraph is worth quoting in full:

John the Apostle migrated from Palestine and lived in Ephesus, where, true to character as a Son of Thunder, he composed apocalyptic works. These, together with his advancing years, the death of the apostles, and predictions such as Mark 9:1, not unnaturally gave rise to the common belief that he would survive to the *parousia*. A man of commanding influence, he gathered about him a number of pupils. In course of time he died; his death fanned the apocalyptic hopes of some, scandalized others, and induced a few to ponder deeply over the meaning of Christian eschatology. One pupil of the apostle incorporated his written works in the canonical Apocalypse; this was at a date about the close of the life of Domitian—*c.* A.D. 96. Another

[21] See, e.g., R. H. Lightfoot, *St. John's Gospel*, Oxford, 1956, pp. 5-7, following T. W. Manson, *BJRL*, 30, No. 2, 1947, p. 320 n. 1.

[22] Hoskyns, *op. cit.*, pp. 100f.

[23] Dodd, *op. cit.*, pp. 449ff., esp. p. 452. His conclusion is tentative and peripheral to his main theme.

pupil was responsible for the Epistles (possibly I John came from one writer, 2 and 3 John from another). Yet another, a bolder thinker, and one more widely read both in Judaism and Hellenism, produced John 1–20. Comparison with 1, 2 and 3 John shows at once that the evangelist stood apart from the busy and quarrelsome ecclesiastical life of the age. Probably he was not popular; probably he died with his gospel still unpublished. It was too original and daring a work for official backing. It was first seized upon by gnostic speculators, who saw the superficial contact which existed between it and their own work; they could at least recognize the language John spoke. Only gradually did the main body of the Church come to perceive that, while John used (at times) the language of gnosticism, his work was in fact the strongest possible reply to the gnostic challenge; that he had beaten the gnostics with their own weapons, and vindicated the permanent validity of the primitive Gospel. The gospel was now edited with chapter 21; the narratives of the final chapter were probably based on traditional material; perhaps material which the evangelist had left but had not worked into the main body of his work. The evangelist, perhaps the greatest theologian in all the history of the church, was now forgotten. His name was unknown. But he had put in his gospel references to the beloved disciple—the highly honored apostle who years before had died in Ephesus. These were now partly understood, and partly misunderstood. It was perceived that they referred to John the son of Zebedee, but wrongly thought that they meant that this apostle was the author of the gospel. 21:24 was now composed on the model of 19:35, and the book was sent out on its long career as the work of John, foe of heretics and beloved of his Lord.[24]

[24] Barrett, *op. cit.*, pp. 113f.

Barrett puts this forward as a hypothesis and admits that it is incapable of proof. He does not use it as a premise from which to interpret the gospel but as a series of tentative conclusions arrived at after the gospel has been interpreted. Bultmann provides no introduction to his commentary, and therefore he devotes no considered discussion to the authorship of the gospel. On the whole, however, he appears to take a similar view to Dodd and Barrett, except that for him the affinities of the evangelist's thought are oriental-gnostic rather than Hellenistic.

2. DATE

On the question of the date of the gospel, even the more radical scholars have been compelled to abandon the middle of the second century as the *terminus ad quem*. Such a date is no longer tenable since the discovery of the so-called Roberts fragment [25] which puts it beyond doubt that the fourth gospel was already in circulation in Egypt between 125 and 140, and, if anything, during the earlier rather than the later part of that period. Sufficient time must be allowed for the gospel to reach Egypt from Ephesus, its normally agreed provenance [26] and to establish itself. It is normal to postulate a generation for that process. Thus a date close to

[25] C. H. Roberts, *An Unpublished Fragment of the Fourth Gospel in the John Rylands Library*, Manchester, 1935. *Fragments of an Unknown Gospel*, ed., H. I. Bell and T. C. Skeat, London, 1935.

[26] The association of the gospel with Ephesus rests entirely on the external evidence of Irenaeus. Attempts have been made from time to time to suggest an Alexandrian provenance, e.g., J. N. Sanders, *The Fourth Gospel in the Second Century*, Cambridge, 1943. Sanders later revised his opinion (*The Foundations of the Christian Faith*, London, 1950, pp. 161f.). W. Bauer, *Das Johannesevangelium*, Tübingen, 1925, favored a Syrian provenance. There is much to be said for this suggestion, but it would still require time for the gospel to find its way into Egypt before 125–140.

A.D. 100 (which is exactly where Westcott put it, despite his adherence to the traditional authorship) does not seem far wrong.[27] Even Bultmann accepts this, and it is curious that Barrett still puts the *terminus ad quem* at 140.[28] This is undoubtedly too late, and the trend of opinion since 1951, whether conservative or radical, is against him.

3. SOURCES

When Streeter wrote the section on the fourth gospel in his *Four Gospels* the quest for written sources was still the order of the day, as it was in synoptic studies. Streeter himself, as we have already noted, maintained the fourth evangelist actually knew and used at least Mark and Luke; and it was widely, if not universally, agreed that he used Mark. In 1938, however, P. Gardner-Smith published a slim, but important and widely influential study,[29] in which he demonstrated (conclusively, to the mind of the present writer) the complete independence of John from all the synoptists, Mark included. It is interesting to find that between his lectures in Cambridge in 1937 and the publication of his book in 1954 (see above, p. 105 and n. 15) C. H. Dodd changed his mind on that question. In 1937 he told us that he accepted John's use of Mark. In 1954 he denies this.[30] Bultmann also, in his commentary (1941) rejects any dependence of John on Mark. Part of the reason for this shift of opinion is undoubtedly the rise of form criticism with its emphasis on oral transmission. Previously even the slightest verbal resemblances were thought to be sufficient to warrant the conclusion of direct literary dependence. The trend today is to require a high percentage of verbal agreement plus agreement in order be-

---

[27] See, however, the views discussed below, p. 131.   [28] Barrett, *op. cit.*, p. 108.
[29] *St. John and the Synoptic Gospels*, Cambridge.   [30] Dodd, *op. cit.*, p. 449.

fore concluding literary dependence. Here again Barrett, although he mentions Gardner-Smith's work,[31] is out of step with the current trend, for he still believes that John knew Mark and Luke.[32]

Quite a new and suggestive approach to the question of sources is found in Bultmann's commentary. He distinguishes between three different classes of material to be found in the fourth gospel. First, there is the "signs source"—which for convenience we will call Σ. This Book of Signs contained a collection of rather crass miracle stories and perhaps other narrative material. Then there is a source which he identifies as "Revelation discourses" (*Offenbarungsreden*). Since these consist of speeches (*logia*) we will call this source Λ. Characteristically, Bultmann thinks that these revelation discourses originated in gnosticism, and were taken over by the fourth evangelist and put to service in the proclamation of the kerygma. By the method of "style-criticism" Bultmann thinks he is able to distinguish between the original material of this source and the evangelist's editing. We are perhaps rather astonished to find that Bultmann considers this gnostic revelation source written originally in Aramaic—unlike the Σ source and the evangelist's own editorial additions.[33] Thirdly, though it is not clear to Bultmann whether this is a separate source from Σ or a continuation of it, John has his own tradition of the passion narrative which again he has heavily edited [34] in the interests of his theology. Occasionally, as for instance in the dating of the passion in relation to the passover, this source contains material of higher value than the Marcan passion narrative.

[31] Barrett, *op. cit.,* p. 34, n. 1.   [32] *Ibid.,* pp. 34–36.

[33] On the question of Aramaic sources in the fourth gospel, see below, p. 118 and the literature mentioned there.

[34] Contrast Dodd, *op. cit.,* pp. 423ff.

Bultmann's views on the gnostic character of Λ are the most controversial part of this thesis. What evidence is there for the possibility of Aramaic gnostic revelation discourses? The Odes of Solomon, to which Bultmann appeals, are not discourses, but hymn-like material in verse form. On the other hand only the prologue of St. John is obviously in verse form—and it is only the prologue which offers a sure basis for distinguishing between the original source and the evangelist's additions. It is a tall order to extend the same operation to the discourses throughout the gospel. Moreover—and this is a characteristic post-Bultmannian objection—is the evangelist merely a commentator? Is he not a creative author in his own right? How can we reduce such a highly individual thinker to the status of a redactor whose prosaic comments interrupt the poetic flow of the original thought? Such are the objections which have been raised against Bultmann's theory by both Käsemann [35] and Haenchen.

That there is considerable pre-Johannine material imbedded in the discourses is becoming increasingly apparent. Two recent studies have been devoted to a study of this pre-Johannine tradition. In 1954 a Danish scholar, Bent Noack,[36] put forward strong grounds for believing that the discourse material as well as the narrative portions of the gospel enshrine traditions which are parallel to, but independent of, the synoptic tradition. Three years later Siegfried Schulz published an important study [37] of the Son of man, Son of God and paraklete logia in the discourses. In the sayings ex-

---

[35] In his essay "Neutestamentliche Fragen von heute." See above, p. 56, n. 2.

[36] B. Noack, *Zur Johanneischen Tradition*, Copenhagen, 1954.

[37] *Untersuchungen zur Menschensohn-Christologie im Johannes-Evangelium*, Göttingen, 1957. Schulz has followed up this work with a more comprehensive study of the tradition behind the discourses in *Komposition und Herkunft der Johanneischen Reden*, 1960.

amined he unravels three strata. The earliest he designates "apocalyptic." Here Jesus is identified with the apocalyptic Son of man who is to come again as the future judge and deliverer at the End. If we tie this in with Tödt's later investigations into the Son of man logia in the synoptic tradition (see above, p. 38, n. 27), this stratum may be assigned to the earliest Aramaic speaking church. This conclusion would appear to be warranted from Schulz's observations on the linguistic features of the logia in this earliest stratum. Secondly, there is what he calls the "neo-interpretation" of the Son of man tradition in a "gnostic" sense. The term "gnostic" used in this connection raises many unsolved problems connected with the so-called gnostic redeemer myth (see below, pp. 121ff.). But the character of this re-interpretation at least is clear: Jesus is presented already in his earthly life as the incarnate Son of man, already exercising the functions of the eschatological judge and redeemer. It would be interesting to explore, in the light of Tödt's conclusions (see above, p. 39), how far this re-interpretation also may be assigned to the early Palestinian tradition, which also contains sayings in which Jesus is in his ministry the present Son of man. The difference between Q and this Johannine stratum appears to be that in the Q sayings the Son of man is used to designate Jesus' present authority in his ministry, with none of the transcendental functions of the eschatological Son of man, whereas in the Johannine sayings Jesus is already exercising the transcendental functions of judgment and salvation. Also the Johannine Son of man is a pre-existent Being who descends to earth. Here is a subject for further investigation. As for the third stratum, the evangelist's own specific contribution, Schulz has very little to say about it. May it be that the evangelist, in taking over a tradition which represents Jesus as already exercising in his earthly life the functions of the transcendental Son of man, has himself in turn linked this idea to that of pre-existence and incarnation? Clearly, there are many questions here for further investigation.[38]

4. DISPLACEMENT THEORIES

The re-arrangement of the text has long fascinated Johannine scholars. Such a conservative critic as Bernard undertook some re-arrangements, and even Roman Catholic scholars have indulged in this procedure without censure.[39] There is certainly much to be said, e.g., for reversing chapters five and six. This has the advantage of avoiding the interruption of the Galilean ministry for a visit to an unspecified feast. The unnamed feast of 5:1 then becomes the passover of 6:4. Equally some dislocation is evident at John 14:31b ("Rise, let us go hence") which is then followed by two more chapters of discourse and the high priestly prayer. On the whole, however, with the notable exception of Bultmann, who rather inconveniently for the reader re-arranges his whole commentary according to his own plan, there is less tendency to favor such attempts today. The trouble is that there has never been any precise agreement on re-arrangements. This is due to the lack of any objective criteria for re-arrangement. F. R. Hoare attempted to furnish such an objective criterion by a calculation of the exact number of letters per page to the original autograph. Unfortunately, however, he had to assume part of what he set out to prove.[40] C. H. Dodd, for instance, explains the apparent dislocations as "phenomena

[38] The present writer hopes to pursue this subject further in a projected work on the Christology of the New Testament.

[39] F. R. Hoare, *The Original Order and Chapters of St. John's Gospel*, London, 1944.

[40] See the present writer's review of Hoare's work (n. 39, above) in *Theology*, 48, May, 1945, pp. 117f.

of composition," while W. F. Howard similarly regarded the fourth gospel as an unfinished product.[41] Here Barrett's observation is typical of the current trend of opinion: "Neither displacement nor redaction theories are needed to explain the present state of the gospel, in which certain roughnesses undoubtedly remain, together with an undoubted impression of a vigorous unity of theme." [42]

It is also interesting to find Käsemann reacting negatively to Bultmann's re-arrangements of the text. The whole procedure, he thinks, is too subjective and ends by making the evangelist say what Bultmann thinks he ought to have said!

5. PAULINISM IN JOHN?

The relation between Paul and John was much discussed by the older liberals. John was seen as the climax of an evolutionary process leading from Jesus through Paul. This view of Christian origins as a straight-forward evolutionary development has now been generally abandoned. On the one hand it is clear that there were many varieties of Christian thought and life in the New Testament age, and on the other hand much that used to be thought specifically Pauline has turned out to be common apostolic Christianity, whether Palestinian or Hellenistic. As a result few would see specific Pauline influence on the fourth gospel. Barrett's judicious conclusion on this question is worth quoting:

It seems easier to believe that Paul and John wrote independently of each other than that John was expressing Pauline theology in narrative form. John was no deutero-Paulinist! Both he and Paul were dependent upon the

[41] *The Fourth Gospel in Recent Criticism and Interpretation*, London, 1931, p. 141.
[42] Barrett, *op. cit.*, p. 20.

primitive tradition. It may however be added that the Johannine theology presupposes the existence of the Pauline.[43]

The specific problems which provoked the distinctively Pauline discussions are notably absent from the Johannine writings. The antithesis between law and gospel is faintly echoed in John 1:17, but there *nomos* means the whole Old Testament revelation, not the "law of commandments contained in ordinances," as it does in Paul. Paul's key term, the "righteousness of God," is strikingly absent from the fourth gospel. John is little interested in the concept of redemptive history (*Heilsgeschichte*) as a thread running from Adam through Moses to Christ. He does not speak of the church as the body of Christ: John 2:21 is often expounded in the Pauline sense, but it probably refers to the literal body of Jesus which passed through death to resurrection. The term *ecclesia* is notably absent from the fourth gospel, its place being taken by the images of the flock (John 10) and the vine (John 15) to denote the religious fellowship established by Jesus. There is very little use of the Old Testament as scriptural proof. One can for instance go through pages of the Nestle text and notice singularly few passages in thick type denoting Old Testament citations. The exceptions (e.g., John 2:17, 12:15, 38–40) are probably derived from the evangelist's sources. Confirmatory evidence of this tendency within the Johannine school is supplied by the lack of Old Testament material in the First Epistle of John. There are of course common elements in Paul and John. There is the same advanced type of Christology, in which the Son of God is the pre-existent agent of creation who then becomes incarnate in Jesus (John 1:1–14; Col. 1:15). Bultmann, of course, attributes this to a common borrowing of the gnostic redeemer

---

[43] *Ibid.*, p. 49.

myth. An alternative closer to hand would be to derive it from the wisdom Christology, which is not specifically Pauline, but found also in Heb. 1:1ff.

6. AN ARAMAIC ORIGIN?

In the early twenties C. F. Burney and C. C. Torrey independently published works claiming an Aramaic origin for the fourth gospel.[44] In its extreme form the theory of an Aramaic original has failed to carry general conviction. But Barrett is surely wrong in rejecting such views as quite unnecessary (here again he is out of step with the trend of opinion). While it is going too far to claim that the whole gospel was originally written in Aramaic, or even (so Bultmann) that the discourses were taken from a (for Bultmann non-Christian, gnostic) Aramaic source, Black's view (see preceding footnote) that there are Aramaic logia enshrined in the discourses would seem wholly justified. Schulz's investigations, as we have seen, tend to support this conclusion. A. M. Hunter has aptly spoken in this connection of a "Johannine Q." [45]

7. JOHANNINE THOUGHT

Of all the subjects discussed in Johannine studies, by far the most controversial is the problem of the affinities of the

[44] C. F. Burney, *The Aramaic Origin of the Fourth Gospel*, Oxford, 1922; C. C. Torrey, "The Aramaic Origin of the Gospel of John," *HTR*, 16, 1923, pp. 305–344. Cf. *Our Translated Gospels* (by the same author), London, 1936; also J. de Zwaan, "John Wrote in Aramaic," *JBL*, 57, 1938, pp. 155–171. For a more cautious treatment, see M. Black, *An Aramaic Approach to the Gospels and Acts*, Oxford, 1946 (first ed.), 1954 (second ed.). Black finds evidences of an Aramaic original at *some* places in the discourses.

[45] *E.T.*, 70, No. 6, p. 165.

evangelist's thought. Some, particularly conservative scholars (e.g., Schlatter, Strack-Billerbeck and to a large extent Hoskyns), stress the Old Testament and Rabbinic background of the Johannine thought. C. H. Dodd and C. K. Barrett, following him, think this is *part* of the background, but find Hellenistic affinities as well. Undoubtedly the older part of the tradition used by the evangelist is Hebraic in origin, but does this cover the later strata, including the evangelist's own contribution? If not, from what milieu do these later strata come?

Some of the older liberals, especially English scholars brought up in the classical tradition, like E. A. Abbott and W. R. Inge, believed that John borrowed heavily from Greek *philosophy,* whether from Platonism or Stoicism. Often it was thought that these influences came to him by way of Philo. Such views immediately suggest themselves from the Johannine prologue with its use of the term Logos, which played such an important part in Greek philosophy. Later the tendency was to stress the evangelist's affinities with Hellenistic *religion.* C. H. Dodd, who, as we have seen, thinks that part of the evangelist's background is Hellenistic, thinks also that it came to him not directly, but *via* a tradition of Hellenistic mysticism of the type found in the later Hermetic literature, to which he produces some remarkable parallels in the fourth gospel. C. K. Barrett similarly stresses the evangelist's religious affinities with Philo and the Hermetic literature.

A very different view of this problem is taken by Bultmann. As has already been indicated on a number of occasions, he thinks that the evangelist has taken over his distinctive theology almost entirely from a gnostic tradition derived ultimately from oriental sources, and has applied that theology to the Christ event. The term gnosticism has been used with various meanings. The older usage followed the second century Christian fathers such as Irenaeus and Hippolytus in restricting it to the great systems of Basilides, Valentinus and their followers. On this definition gnosticism stands for various second century deviations from Christian orthodoxy. Next, it became apparent that gnostic tendencies were already to be found in the New Testament, in the false teachings combatted in the pastorals, the Epistle of Jude, and perhaps even in Colossians. But still it seemed that the false teachings in question were deviations arising from within primitive Christianity. More recently, however, in the History of Religions School,[46] followed by Bultmann and his pupils, the term has come to cover a syncretistic tradition which allegedly arose in the Orient and infiltrated into heterodox Palestinian Judaism (the Dead Sea Scrolls), into the baptist cults of Palestine and Syria, including Mandaism, into Hellenistic Judaism (Philo) and into higher Hellenistic paganism (the Hermetic literature). Neither the tradition behind Philo, nor the Hermetic literature, according to Bultmann, is the source of the Johannine thought; all are derived independently from this common source in oriental gnosticism. This gnosticism had also found its way into various streams of Christianity before John and even before Paul. Not only did Paul combat gnosticizing tendencies in Galatia and Corinth,[47] but his own thinking was influenced by "orthodox" borrowings from gnostic mythology on the part of his Hellenistic predecessors. These borrowings are found in Christology (the gnostic myth of the pre-existent redeemer who became incarnate), in soteriology (the presentation of

[46] Beginning with Reitzenstein and Bousset. For a popular presentation, see Hans Jonas, *The Gnostic Religion*, Boston, 1958.

[47] Colossians and Ephesians also combat the same tendencies, but for Bultmann these epistles are deutero-Pauline.

Christ's death as a victory over the cosmic powers of evil), and in ecclesiology (the concept of the church as the body of Christ). Parallel borrowings from gnostic mythology, according to Bultmann, are also found in the letters of Ignatius of Antioch and also in the Odes of Solomon. Basic to the gnostic outlook was its dualistic view of the world. There was an upper world, eternal, real and good, and a lower world, temporal, unreal and evil. The upper world was the sphere of spirit or *nous* (mind), the lower the sphere of matter. Man belonged by his creation to both orders. Human souls had previously existed in the upper world and it was their misfortune to have become allied with human, material bodies. Creation was in fact the fall of the pre-existent soul. But there was a deliverance available to man already during this earthly life. This could be achieved by the acquisition of "gnosis," knowledge, brought down from the upper world by a heavenly redeemer who came down into the lower world in a kind of pseudo-incarnation. The content of this redeeming knowledge was information about the upper world—what it was like, and the pass-words necessary in order to return there. Those who accepted the revelation were released from the bondage of their material bodies, and their return to the heavenly world at death was assured.

It was, contends Bultmann, precisely from this gnostic redeemer myth that the author of the fourth gospel derived the terms in which he restated the Christian kerygma. This is not to say, however, that the author of the fourth gospel was himself a gnostic. He is, Bultmann asserts, a Christian thinker concerned with the kerygma. He brings his gnostic concepts into captivity to Christ. And he is deliberately writing against non-Christian gnosticism by borrowing their own language and concepts. For he attaches the redeemer myth to the real historical figure of Jesus. *Jesus* is the pre-existent

Son who becomes incarnate, who brings the revelation which is his word. And in his coming he creates a *krisis,* a sifting process. He promises salvation to those who accept his word, and condemnation to those who reject it. He then ascends back at his crucifixion to the heavenly world of light, drawing his "own"—those who have accepted his word—after him. Moreover, not only is this gnostic redeemer myth radically altered by being attached to the historical figure of Jesus, and thus transformed precisely into an interpretation of him, of his person, work and destiny; the gnostic concepts in themselves are profoundly modified by the Biblical-Hebraic outlook of primitive Christianity. The dualism of the fourth gospel is not metaphysical or cosmic, but a dualism of decision, of sin and unbelief on the one hand, of faith and righteousness on the other. There is no pre-existence of the soul. Revelation is not the impartation of secrets about the upper world, but simply *the person of Jesus himself,* in whom one is confronted with the very word of God. Jesus challenges men not to recollect their heavenly origin before their souls entered their mortal bodies, but rather to *faith.* Redemption is not secured at death, as in gnostic eschatology, but already here and now, in the preaching of the Christian kerygma, which is the work of the paraklete. There are, it is true, certain elements in the fourth gospel, which, as Bultmann sees it, do not square with the evangelist's Christian gnosticism. These are the sacramentalism of John 3:5 (rebirth through baptism with *water and* the spirit) and 6:51c–56 (eating the flesh and drinking the blood of the Son of man); and also the futurist eschatology of 5:25–29. These features, which contradict the rest of the evangelist's theology, even in the discourses in which they occur, are, however, assigned to an ecclesiastical redactor, who allegedly touched up the gospel subsequently for use in church. Yet for Bultmann

John is not a mystic, despite his supposed anti-sacramentalism. The life of faith is always a paradox containing a "not yet" as well as an "already." Faith has constantly to be renewed in decision and obedience, in the keeping of the commandments, in love (*agape*) for the brethren.

Bultmann's elimination of the sacramental references and of the futurist eschatology has not secured assent outside his own school. Oscar Cullmann [48] and Alf Correll [49] find a sacramental background not only in the usual places (John 3:1-21; 6:22-65) but throughout the signs and discourses, while Correll argues that the futurist eschatology is integral to the evangelist's presentation. Here, however, we are concerned with the reaction which Bultmann's commentary has found within his own school. In the main, his position is accepted, though there is criticism of some of the details.

They think that Bultmann has attributed to John too much of his own ideas. It is much more likely that the evangelist himself accepted the historicity of the miracles he records: they were not for him, just symbolic stories, as Bultmann thinks. Pre-existence is "mythologically" important for the evangelist. It is not simply a device for reinforcing the transcendental origin of the word which Jesus brings. Nor should the futurist eschatology be completely eliminated as the work of the ecclesiastical redactor. There *is* futurist eschatology in John, albeit in a weakened form. We would agree with all these criticisms. The curious thing, however, is the way his pupils accept without question the theory of the pre-Christian redemption myth. We readily grant that there is in Johannine thought a "plus" which cannot be explained from the Old Testament, from late Judaism or from the earliest kerygma. We are ready to agree, as all indica-

[48] *Early Christian Worship*, tr., A. S. Todd and J. B. Torrance, London, 1953.
[49] *Consummatum Est*, London, 1959.

tions now are increasingly tending to suggest, that gnosticism or whatever we choose to call it is a widespread phenomenon antedating the beginnings of Christianity; that it had already infiltrated into Judaism, both Palestinian-sectarian and Hellenistic; and that from these sources it had in turn supplied elements to Christian theology even before John. But the theory of a pre-Christian gnostic redeemer myth rests entirely on sources which are found either within the New Testament itself or which are later than the New Testament. In fact, Bultmann's chief "evidence" [50] lies in the Johannine discourses themselves, in which he believes he has by style-criticism distinguished the pre-Johannine sources from the evangelist's comments.

Therefore it is equally possible that the so-called gnostic redeemer myth, which is only found in gnostic writings later than the fourth gospel, is actually a deviation originating from within Christianity itself. The gnostics were of course exposed to extraneous influences, and it was precisely these influences that made them heretical. But their pre-existent redeemer myth seems on purely chronological grounds to be derived from the Christian writings themselves. It is hoped that the newly discovered gnostic documents from Hammadi [51] will throw more light on the vexed question of gnostic origins, and give some guide to what pre-Christian gnosticism actually contained. But since these documents, on all showing, are none of them earlier than the second century A.D., and since all of them have some connection with Christianity, however tenuous, it is hard to see how they can

[50] As he reiterated in a conversation with the present writer at Marburg in October, 1961.

[51] See G. Quispel, H. C. Puech, W. C. van Unnik, *The Jung Codex*, London, 1955; A. Guillaumont *et al., The Gospel of Thomas*, London, 1959; M. Malinine *et al., Evangelium Veritatis*, Zurich, 1956; W. C. van Unnik, *Newly Discovered Gnostic Writings*, London and Naperville, 1960.

clear up our major problem—the existence of a gnostic redeemer myth in pre-Christian times. It has been claimed [52]
that Bultmann's view on the matter has been refuted. This
is not so. It still remains possible. If we reject it, we do so
not because we think that it in any way undermines the
truth of the Christian kerygma. After all, the earlier concepts
employed by the kerygma were equally mythological, though
the mythology from which they were derived was Jewish
apocalyptic. Bultmann's theory, far from undermining the
authority of the fourth gospel, actually allows its distinctive
witness to stand out in even sharper relief. This is the great
contribution of Bultmann's commentary. If we reject the
theory of the gnostic redeemer myth we do so on purely
scholarly grounds—that it remains unproven, and that the
chronological evidence weighs heavily against it.

A completely new turn to the debate about the affinities
of the evangelist's thought has been given by the discovery of
the Dead Sea Scrolls. As far as the present writer is aware, it
was K. G. Kuhn of Heidelberg who in a series of articles in
the *Zeitschrift für Theologie und Kirche* [53] first pointed out
the striking similarities both of thought and language between some of the newly discovered sectarian literature, especially the Manual of Discipline, and the Johannine literature. Kuhn contends that the scrolls exhibit a dualism derived
ultimately from Iranian religion. There is the same series of
contrasts between good and evil, light and darkness, truth
and falsehood. It is an ethical and eschatological, not a metaphysical, dualism; but, as compared with its Iranian source,
it has been profoundly modified by the Old Testament faith

---

[52] Van Unnik, *op. cit.*, pp. 92f.

[53] "Die in Palästina gefundenen hebräischen Texte und das Neue Testament,"
ZThK, 47, 1950, pp. 192–211; "πειρασμός etc.," *ZThK*, 49, 1952, pp. 200–222;
"Die Sektenschrift und die iranische Religion," *ibid.*, pp. 296–316.

in God as Creator. God has created *both* good and evil, *both* light and darkness, *both* truth and falsehood. Yet the dualism itself represents a distinct "plus" as compared with the Old Testament: "This dualistic ideology is totally alien to Old Testament thought, nor can it be interpreted as an outgrowth of the Old Testament." [54] Now it is precisely these same pairs of opposites, modified in the same way by the Old Testament faith in God as Creator, precisely the same ethical and eschatological (though not metaphysical) dualism which we find in the Johannine literature. Moreover we find the same dualistic vocabulary, such as "spirit of truth," "spirit of falsehood," "sons of light" (John 12:36, IQS 1:9, 3:24f.), "light of life" (John 8:12, IQS 3:7), "he who walks in darkness" (John 12:35, IQS 3:21). At the same time there is an important difference: in the Qumran literature the good, truth, light, etc., are always present in the universe. In the fourth gospel they are introduced as eschatological possibilities by the coming of Christ. Many scholars have been impressed by Kuhn's suggestions and have carried them further.[55] Bo Reicke defined the type of religious syncretism in the scrolls and in the Johannine literature as "pre-

---

[54] *Ibid.*, p. 303.

[55] Among experts on the Dead Sea Scrolls we may mention the following: M. Burrows, *The Dead Sea Scrolls*, New York, 1955; W. F. Albright, "Recent Discoveries in Palestine and the Gospel of St. John" in *The Background of the New Testament and the Eschatology*, pp. 153–171 (see p. 2, n. 3). Among New Testament scholars: O. Cullmann, "The Significance of the Qumran Texts for Research into the Beginnings of Christianity," *JBL*, 74, 1951, pp. 213–226, reprinted in *The Scrolls and the New Testament*, ed., Krister Stendahl, New York, 1957; and (by the same author) "A New Approach to the Interpretation of the Fourth Gospel," *E.T.*, 71, No. 1, 1959, pp. 8–12, No. 2, pp. 39–43; B. Reicke, "Traces of Gnosticism in the Dead Sea Scrolls?" *NTS*, 1, 1954, pp. 137–141; R. E. Brown (Roman Catholic), "The Qumran Scrolls and the Johannine Gospel and Epistles." See also the reports of A. M. Hunter, *E.T.*, 71, No. 6, pp. 164–167, No. 7, pp. 219–222, and of C. Leslie Mitton, *ibid.*, No. 11, pp. 337–340.

gnosticism." Cullmann has put forward the thesis that the discovery of the scrolls has so widened our knowledge of Palestinian Judaism that the picture of primitive Christianity which has been generally accepted since the days of F. C. Baur and the Tübingen school must be radically revised. In the Tübingen scheme, it will be remembered, the development of Christianity was presented in three phases: Jewish Christianity, Hellenistic Christianity and early catholicism. Now it appears that much that was previously thought to be Hellenistic is to be found already in sectarian Palestinian Christianity, in particular the type of tradition found in the fourth gospel. With this much we are prepared to agree. But Cullmann goes further and propounds the thesis that this strain first entered primitive Christianity with Stephen and the Hellenists (Acts 6 and 7). The term "Hellenists" means, he suggests, not "Greek-speaking Jews of the diaspora," as commonly interpreted, but sectarian, or as he prefers to call them, "non-conformist" Palestinian Jews. Cullmann finds the link between these Hellenists and the sectarian Jews of Qumran in their common critical attitude towards the temple at Jerusalem. It was the Hellenists, he suggests, who evangelized Samaria, and through them that the sectarian tradition of Palestinian Judaism passed into the Johannine school. The evidence for this he deduces from John 4, particularly the saying, "others have labored, and you have entered into their labor" (verse 38). The same tradition, he contends, also underlies the Epistle to the Hebrews, which is also radically opposed to the Jewish Temple. This thesis is brilliant and suggestive, but not altogether convincing. In the first place, all the Hellenists we know of have Greek rather than Palestinian names (Acts 6:5). Their Bible, if we are to trust Acts 7, appears to have been the Septuagint rather than the Hebrew Old Testament. The evidence for their theological outlook is tenuous, for we do not know where the author of Acts derived the material for Stephen's speech in Acts 7, if we assume that it is not a Lucan composition. Moreover, Stephen's criticism of the temple, as Cullmann himself admits, is far more radical than that of Qumran. The Qumraners were critical not of the temple as such, but of the priestly party who ran it. Stephen, however, regards the temple as wrong from the start: even in Old Testament times its very erection and maintenance was a signal act of faithlessness and disobedience on the part of Israel. The fourth gospel's attitude to the temple on the other hand is closer to that of Qumran. The temple as an institution was legitimate during Israel's history, but now that the Christ has come it has been superseded (John 2:19–21, 4:21–24).

It is still too early to say whether the thesis will establish itself that the Johannine "plus" can be adequately accounted for as a development of sectarian Judaism. Barrett, as we have already seen, was unable to take account of the Qumran material in his discussion of the non-Christian background, since his work was finished in 1951, too early for an assessment of the Qumran material. He does, as mentioned, state in a footnote to his preface, written in 1955, that it would not "have substantially modified" his work.[56] In other words, he still adheres to the view that the source of the Johannine "plus" is to be sought in the higher paganism of the Hellenistic world. Bultmann, similarly, in the third (German) edition of his *Theology of the New Testament*, sees no reason to modify his view that the Johannine "plus" is derived from oriental gnosticism. He and his school[57] are impressed by the absence of the gnostic redeemer myth from

---

[56] Barrett, *op. cit.*, p. viii, n. 1.

[57] Cf. Käsemann in "Neutestamentliche Fragen von heute," *ZThK*, 54, 1957, pp. 17ff.

the Qumran material. This is for them conclusive proof that the Qumran material cannot be the *direct* source of the Johannine "plus." Rather, both Qumran and the Johannine literature represent independent derivations from oriental gnosticism. If, however, as we are inclined to believe, the whole notion of a pre-Christian gnostic redeemer myth is merely an unproven assumption of the History of Religions School, for which there is no pre-Christian evidence (see above, p. 124), this objection falls to the ground. The question therefore remains, how did the Palestinian sectarian tradition find its way into the Johannine tradition? The present writer is inclined to the view that it came in through the Baptist sect, which we know existed at Ephesus (Acts 19:1-7) and against which the fourth evangelist so obviously polemizes in the early chapters of his gospel (John 1:6-8, 15, 19-42; 3:22-30). This sect revered John the Baptist as the bringer of a gnostic type of revelation (cf. the language of the Benedictus, Luke 1:77), which it defined in the gnostic terms of light and life. That John the Baptist himself had connections with the Qumran community has already been suggested, notably by John A. T. Robinson.[58] It seems therefore quite plausible to suppose that his later followers borrowed even more heavily from the same tradition to express their growing veneration for their master.

8. THE PALESTINIAN BACKGROUND

In other ways the connections between the fourth gospel and Palestine are becoming increasingly clear. Some of the topography, which in the past has puzzled critics and thrown doubt on the author's (or his tradition's) knowledge of

---

[58] John A. T. Robinson, *Twelve New Testament Studies,* London and Naperville, 1962, pp. 11-27.

Palestine, has been substantiated by archeological discovery. One such puzzle was the location of Aenon near Salim (John 3:23). There is a place called Ainun near Salim by the headwaters of Wadi Far'ah: this substantiates John's statement that "there were many waters there." [59] Joachim Jeremias has given an account of excavations in Jerusalem [60] which resulted in the discovery of the pool of Bethesda (John 5:2ff.). According to Hunter, [61] this has also been confirmed by the copper scroll from Qumran. The excavations at Shechem have made it reasonably certain that Sychar in John 4:5 should be identified with that place. In fact Shechem is the reading of the Old Syriac version at this point, and it is probably correct. Finally, mention should be made of an article by John A. T. Robinson, [62] who studies other aspects of the evangelist's presentation, notably his attitude toward the "Jews," resulting in the conclusion that "The *Heimat* of the Johannine tradition, and the milieu in which it took shape, was the heart of southern Palestine." [63]

Yet another point. There is increasing respect in many quarters for some of the distinctive historical traditions enshrined in the fourth gospel. A notable champion of this tradition, who had no conservative ax to grind, was the French scholar, Maurice Goguel. [64] Hunter [65] lists six points in which he thinks the fourth evangelist provides sound historical traditions to supplement or correct the synoptists:

1. Two of Jesus' disciples were formerly disciples of John the Baptist (John 1:35–42).

[59] Hunter, *op. cit.*, p. 165.

[60] *Die Wiederentdeckung von Bethesda*, Göttingen, 1949. Cf. also *Unknown Sayings of Jesus*, tr., R. H. Fuller, London, 1964, pp. 54f.

[61] Hunter, *loc. cit.*   [62] *NTS*, 6/2 (1960), pp. 117–131.   [63] *Ibid.*, p. 124.

[64] M. Goguel, *Jésus*, Paris, 1950 (second ed.).   [65] Hunter, *op. cit.*, p. 219.

2. The Judean ministry of Jesus prior to the Galilean ministry (John 3:22 filling the gap implied by Mark 1:14a).

3. The Messianic crisis following the feeding of the multitude (John 6:15, perhaps implied by Mark 6:45: Jesus forces his disciples to leave, while he dismisses the crowd).

4. An extended Judean ministry during the last six months, with an interval of retirement (John 7:14–11:54: the synoptists also contain hints of a more extended ministry at Jerusalem).

5. The dating of the Last Supper on 14 rather than 15 Nisan. This dating is still widely accepted, despite Jeremias' valiant attempts to vindicate the Marcan chronology.

6. Jesus before Annas as the power behind the high priestly throne (18:13).

Some of these traditions have more claim to validity than others, but none is historically impossible.

It is not surprising that quite responsible scholars, and not only those with conservative predilections who would naturally be inclined to "cash in" on the new evidence, are beginning seriously to entertain the possibility that the fourth gospel was written much earlier than has been commonly supposed. If Gardner-Smith is right in denying any dependence on the synoptists a date around 80 or even earlier becomes possible (so Hunter). The Aramaic and Palestinian affinities of the author re-open the possibility of a closer connection with John the Apostle than the dominant critical opinion has allowed (so Mitton). If the idiom of thought is so thoroughly Palestinian (albeit sectarian), might not the teaching of the fourth gospel go back ultimately to Jesus himself (so again Mitton)? It seems to the present writer that these three possibilities are hazardous in the extreme, and great caution is advised. The fatal objection is that the Q material is our earliest (some of it perhaps with a pre-resurrection *Sitz im Leben* [66]) evidence for the teaching of Jesus. It presents him as the proclaimer of the kingdom of God: the fourth gospel on the other hand completes the process tentatively initiated by the synoptists by presenting Jesus as the proclaimer of himself: it represents the culmination of the radical reassessment of Jesus in the light of the Easter event and the church's experience of the risen Christ. Barrett's views on the origin of the fourth gospel, modified in the light of the Qumran discoveries as we have suggested above (p. 129), would still seem best to fit the state of the evidence.

[66] See Heinz Schürmann (above, p. 75, n. 12).

VIII

Diagnosis and Prospect

To DON THE MANTLE of a prophet and venture to predict how New Testament studies will develop in the ensuing decade would be a very hazardous attempt, which no one in his senses would undertake. It is true, as Paul Schubert observed some years ago, that "diagnoses and prognoses are frequently made in all fields of research," [1] and that such attempts have been made from time to time throughout the first half of the present century. No doubt a very discerning observer in 1914 might have predicted the rise of form criticism from

[1] *The Study of the New Testament Today and Tomorrow,* ed., Harold R. Willoughby, Chicago, 1947, p. 209, n. 1. See also the literature named by Schubert covering the period from 1903 to 1946.

the work of Wrede and Wellhausen on the gospels and of Gunkel on the Pentateuch. He might also have predicted from the work of Johannes Weiss and Albert Schweitzer that the importance of apocalyptic eschatology for the understanding of Jesus' mission and message would be generally accepted. From this he could have concluded that the liberal Protestant portrait of Jesus was doomed. But this might have tempted him to predict the triumph of the History of Religions School, and the resultant loss of the New Testament's relevance for the modern world. He could never have predicted Karl Barth's *Epistle to the Romans* and the consequent recovery of the theological, as opposed to the purely historical, interpretation of the Old Testament. Again, a discerning observer might have detected from the writings of Bultmann during the period 1925-29 the trends which eventually produced the essay, "The New Testament and Mythology," in 1941,[2] but he could hardly have foreseen that it would again alter the whole atmosphere of New Testament studies after the Second World War, making them once more analytic and critical, rather than synthetic and conservative. Again, once this new ascendency of Bultmann had established itself in the forties, our observer in 1950 might have predicted that that ascendency would evoke a "change of fronts" in which conservative scholars would renew the quest of the historical Jesus, but he could hardly have foreseen Käsemann's essay of 1953, which reopened the quest within the Bultmann circle itself. Past experience suggests therefore that all prognostications are at best limited and fallible. "Miracles" may always happen, like Barth's *Epistle to the Romans,* Bultmann's "New Testament and Mythology" or Käsemann's "Die Frage nach dem histori-

---

[2] See R. Bultmann, *Existence and Faith,* New York, 1960, and the introduction by Schubert M. Ogden.

schen Jesus." And who knows what new knowledge may emerge from the Qumran or Nag Hammadi discoveries, or from others that may yet occur?

AN EMERGING CONSENSUS

We will therefore content ourselves with a more modest role than that of the prophet. First, we will pick out from our preceding investigations those trends which in our opinion promise to meet with general acceptance, and then underline certain unresolved problems which represent urgent tasks for future study.

Among current trends which ought to secure general recognition we would first note the rejection of recent sporadic attempts to dislodge the two-document hypothesis as a working presupposition in synoptic studies. In the two dominant concerns in this field, the resumed quest of the historical Jesus and the new concern for the evangelists as theologians in their own right, the priority of Mark and the existence of the Q tradition are now generally being taken for granted.

Secondly, we may expect that the form critical method will come to be more widely accepted as one of the indispensable tools for the study of the pre-literary tradition behind our written gospels. British scholars in particular have been inclined to take it for a tool of "limited utility," to restrict its operation to the mere classification of the material, and to deny its capacity to make historical judgments. The post-Bultmannians should relieve their fears that the thorough-going acceptance of this method necessarily results in excessive historical skepticism about Jesus.[3] To take one ex-

[3] Cf. *The Christ of Faith and the Jesus of History* by A. G. Herbert, London, 1962, esp. pp. 33–38.

ample: when we have eliminated all of the Messianic titles
as self-designations from the authentic logia of Jesus, the
substance of a Messianic self-understanding is still implicitly
present in the words and deeds of Jesus. There is no need to
defend the historicity of these titles by arbitrarily limiting the
application of the form critical method at this point as
Cullmann has done in his New Testament Christology.

Third, we may look for growing consensus among scholars,
whether conservative or radical, that the historical Jesus
is both relevant and necessary to the kerygma. Despite
Bultmann's brave attempt to prove that for the kerygma
only the bare facticity (the *Dass*) of Jesus matters, the trend
on all sides is to a recognition that the character and content
(the *Was* and the *Wie*) of his history are equally important.
This, as we shall see later, does not mean that we can yet
agree as to the sense in which it is relevant to the kerygma.

Fourth, we may hope for a greater clarification between
the Palestinian and Hellenistic strata in the traditions behind
our written gospels. Much of the material which Bultmann
had assigned to the Hellenistic tradition (e.g., the miracle
stories and the passion predictions) is now being assigned to
Palestinian Christianity. And, as we have seen, much of the
tradition behind the fourth gospel appears to be going the
same way. Indeed, the whole distinction, common since
Bousset, between Palestinian and Hellenistic Christianity is
becoming increasingly problematical. The urgent need is
for a sound clarification of the distinction lest the Hellenistic
contribution be eliminated altogether.

Fifth, in Pauline studies there is a widespread consensus
that Paul's basic kerygma is in substantial agreement with
his predecessors. Paul's original contribution is to be sought,
not in his transformation of Christianity into a redemptive

cult, but on the one hand in the elimination of the law as the means to salvation—a position which he worked out in controversy with the Judaizers—and on the other hand his equal insistence that salvation was not a magically imparted inalienable physical status, but a life which had to be worked out in concrete obedience and which was always characterized by a "not yet," a position which he evolved in opposition to syncretistic Hellenistic religiosity. The unresolved question is the theological environment out of which Paul emerged. Was it Pharisaic (W. D. Davies) or Hellenistic (the Bultmann school) Judaism?

Sixth, there is likely to be increasing recognition that the evangelists are to be taken seriously as theologians in their own right. There is need for much more detailed study of the redactional work of Matthew and Luke of the kind so admirably exhibited by H. J. Held in his study of the Matthean miracles (see above, p. 73, n. 6).

Seventh, there is a growing acceptance of the deutero-Pauline character of Ephesians as well as Pastorals, perhaps even of II Thessalonians and Colossians. But the positive implications of this recognition need to be exploited. It is not enough simply to leave them out of account in our construction of the Pauline theology. These writings must be evaluated as evidence for the development towards early catholicism in the sub-apostolic age. The same holds good for Hebrews and I Peter. It is becoming increasingly clear that the New Testament covers three phases in the emergence of Christianity: the ministry of Jesus, the apostolic and the sub-apostolic ages. Just as we are learning to see the apostolic age as the response to Jesus, in which what was implicit in him is now made explicit, so too it should become increasingly apparent that the sub-apostolic age, so far from being a corruption of its immediate predecessor, was the legitimate response to the apostolic age, in which what was implicit in the earlier period is now made explicit in the later. This would mean, ultimately, that the second century achievements of catholicism—the creed, canon, episcopate and liturgy—are the unfolding of what was implicit in the apostolic kerygma.

UNRESOLVED PROBLEMS

We have spoken thus far of current trends which we have ventured to expect will find increasing and general acceptance. We turn now to the unresolved problems.

The first of these, as we have already indicated, concerns the place of Jesus' history in the kerygma. In their legitimate reaction against Bultmann's treatment of the history of Jesus merely as a factual peg upon which to hang the kerygma, some post-Bultmannians are moving to the opposite position that the kerygma is simply a means whereby we are brought to encounter with the historical Jesus. We have already noted J. M. Robinson's contention that the modern historical method has given us an access to the historical Jesus that is an *equivalent alternative* to the traditional access which the Christian church has had to him, since the first Easter, in the kerygma. This might imply that the *sole* purpose of the kerygma is to give us access to the historical Jesus. This possibility becomes fully implicit in H. Braun's article on primitive Christianity:

When Jesus is known as the One who did not abide in death, as the One who was soon to come again, this means that precisely for the first recipients of the (Easter) visions and for those who first held this faith—in face of the catastrophe of the cross—that all they had learnt from Jesus had been validated ("All das in Kraft gesetzt worden, was sie von Jesus gelernt hatten").[4]

This means that the kerygmatic proclamation of Jesus as risen from the dead is only a way of continuing after his crucifixion his eschatological proclamation, his radical ethic, and his teaching about God. The danger of a new kind of liberalism, which the present writer feared in his review of J. M. Robinson's *New Quest* (see above, p. 2, n. 2), seems here to be fully realized. Instead of the liberal Protestant historical Jesus who taught the fatherhood of God and the brotherhood of man as the essence of Christianity, we now have a Jesus who proclaims an eschatological message, a radical demand of obedience and a teaching about God as a means of existential encounter. Only if we insist that these three areas of Jesus' proclamation point beyond themselves to God's immediate presence and redemptive action in the person of Jesus can this danger be averted. Otherwise the three areas of Jesus' proclamation become in the last resort detachable from his person just as the teaching of the liberal Protestant Jesus was ultimately detachable from his person. With this proviso we may see in Braun's position an improvement upon the near kerygmatic-docetism of Bultmann: it brings the character and content, as well as the bare facticity of Jesus' history into the kerygma. But is it an adequate characterization of the kerygma? Is the purpose of the kerygma *merely* to produce an encounter with the historical Jesus? As we saw in our discussion of Bultmann's lecture to the Heidelberg Academy (see above, pp. 46–53) there is a *plus* in God's eschatological action since Good Friday and Easter Day which makes the historical Jesus—the pre-Good

[4] *RGG,* third ed., I, s.v. "Christentum, I, Entstehung," col. 1689.

Friday Jesus—out of date. The pre-Good Friday historical Jesus proclaimed that in himself God was beginning his eschatological action and was about to consummate that action. The post-Easter kerygma proclaims that in Jesus' life, death and resurrection God *has* (note the difference of tenses) acted eschatologically, although that action still has to be rounded off in the future. This interpretation of the kerygma which we have proposed avoids the Scylla of neo-liberalism and the Charybdis of kerygmatic docetism, and, we would contend, is a truer characterization of the New Testament kerygma itself. But it is open, from a post-Bultmannian point of view, to a fatal objection of its own. It can state the eschatological action of God in quantitative terms, in phases of *Heilsgeschichte,* and therefore in the last resort only non-existentially and with a false objectification. This objection can only be sustained if, as we have contended (see above, pp. 21–24) there are significant areas in the kerygma which do not lend themselves to an existential interpretation. Clearly, the problem of the place of the historical Jesus in the kerygma has not yet been solved.

Closely associated with this problem is the rift which has appeared in the early Palestinian kerygma itself. In some Palestinian circles, as evidenced by the Q material,[5] by one stratum of the Marcan passion predictions [6] and by the

---

[5] The Q material contains neither logia referring to the passion, nor a passion narrative. But, Tödt maintains, the very fact that it continues Jesus' own proclamation after its validity had been radically called in question by his death shows that it presumes the interpretation of his death given above. The explicit identification of the earthly Jesus with the Son of man also presumes this vindication, and is intended to express it. (*The Son of Man in the Synoptic Tradition,* pp. 235–250.)

[6] Mark 8:31, 9:12, 9:31, 10:33f. The references to the "deliverance" of Jesus into the hands of "men" and the allusions to his "rejection," derived from Ps. 118:22, signify the interpretation of the cross as man's No to Jesus and his message. See Tödt, *op. cit.,* pp. 144–157.

kerygmatic material in the sermons in Acts,[7] the death of Jesus is interpreted as Israel's No to the proclamation of Jesus and the resurrection as God's Yes, his validation of Jesus' message (cf. Braun's understanding of the kerygma above). In other Palestinian circles, or in the same circles at a slightly later date, the death of Jesus is interpreted in terms of Isa. 53 as an atoning death for sin.[8] Here the passion of Jesus is interpreted not as an act of sinful man, or not only as such, but as, or also as, one of the redemptive acts of God. Is this an alteration or addition to the original kerygma? Is it an alternative form of the kerygma, which, however, is really saying the same thing as the No-Yes interpretation of the cross and resurrection? Here is an unsolved problem which vitally affects the unity of the New Testament. It is clear that our triumph at the recovery of the unity of the New Testament in the kerygma [9] was premature. While it remains true that the kerygma is basic to all of the New Testament writings, it is less clear than it was that the kerygma is identical throughout. It is not simply that there are varying expressions of the one kerygma: there are, apparently, variations in the substance of the kerygma itself. Here, then, is another urgent task for New Testament

---

[7] Acts 2:23f., 2:36, 3:14f., 4:10f. (note the quotation from Ps. 118:22), 5:30, 10:39f., 13:29f.

[8] Mark 10:45, 14:24 and the kerygma quoted by and presumed in the Pauline writings (e.g., I Cor. 15:3, Rom. 4:25). The attempt of M. D. Hooker to eliminate the influence of Isa. 53 entirely from the synoptic gospels (*Jesus and the Servant*, Greenwich, 1959), supported by C. K. Barrett, "The Background of Mark 10:45," in *New Testament Essays in Memory of T. W. Manson*, ed., H. J. B. Higgins, Manchester, 1959, is unconvincing. See the review of Miss Hooker's book by J. Jeremias in *JTS*, n.s. 11, pp. 140ff.; also Tödt, *op. cit.*

[9] See, e.g., A. M. Hunter, *The Unity of the New Testament*, London, 1943, especially Chapter II, which demonstrates that the kerygma underlies all the books of the New Testament.

scholarship—to explore the relations between these variations in the kerygma.

All this is no doubt very confusing for the non-expert, who demands "assured results," particularly when the matter under discussion is the title deeds of the Christian faith, and when the non-expert himself is a Christian believer. He does not want his faith to be tied down to what the professors tell him is true at any given moment. It is not, however, to the professors that he goes to know about the object of his faith: what he believes in is Christ as he is proclaimed by the living church today. Yet this Christ is not a myth, but the Jesus of Nazareth in whom, according to the kerygma and to faith, God has acted decisively for man's redemption. Historical investigation therefore has an important, though subordinate, role to play in connection with Christian faith. It is important since faith makes a claim with respect to a figure of history, and historical investigation is necessary to show that that figure can support the claims made for him. But it is subordinate, since historical investigation cannot in the nature of the case validate the claim that kerygma and faith make for him. Similarly, the church is a human society, of which the kerygma and faith claim that it is the eschatological community. Since it is a historical society, its history, including its beginnings, is open to historical investigation. But historical investigation can never demonstrate that the church is the eschatological community. Once again, historical research has an important, though subordinate, role to play in relation to faith. The Christian believer does not therefore have to wait for the professors to tell him what he has to believe, nor need he fear because the professors are always changing their minds or disagreeing among themselves. He can only look to them to clarify the issues involved in the historical aspect of a faith which, though historical, nevertheless transcends history.

Index of Scripture References

Index of Authors